VETERANS ADMINISTRATION HOSPITALS

Evaluative Studies

This series of studies seeks to bring about greater understanding and promote continuing review of the activities and functions of the federal government. Each study focuses on a specific program, evaluating its cost and efficiency, the extent to which it achieves its objectives, and the major alternative means— public and private—for reaching those objectives. Yale Brozen, professor of economics at the University of Chicago and an adjunct scholar of the American Enterprise Institute for Public Policy Research, is the director of the program.

VETERANS ADMINISTRATION HOSPITALS

An economic analysis of government enterprise

Cotton M. Lindsay

American Enterprise Institute for Public Policy Research
Washington, D. C.

ISBN 0-8447-3185-4

Evaluative Studies 23, November 1975

Library of Congress Catalog Card No. 75-29828

Cover maze reproduced with permission from Maze Craze
© 1971 Troubadour Press, San Francisco

CONTENTS

CHAPTER I

OVERVIEW

Economists ask three questions about government institutions such as the Veterans Administration (VA) hospital system: (1) What is the institution's perceived role or function? (2) What is it doing—that is, is it fulfilling this role efficiently? (3) Is the role itself well considered? This study of the VA hospital system seeks to discover answers to each of these questions.

One cannot, however, discuss this topic in a vacuum. The VA hospital system is part of a vast, costly, and growing health care industry in this country, an industry which currently consumes about one-twelfth of the nation's resources. More than $26 billion is spent each year on hospital care alone. In order that each of these questions may be weighed in its proper context, alternative sources of the services provided by VA hospitals must be evaluated. There are, in both private and public sectors, many alternatives to the current organization; no study of the VA system can be complete unless it is accompanied by an evaluation of these institutions which could, to some extent, take its place.

Not surprisingly, the VA hospital system has achieved its major growth in periods immediately after this country has been at war. It was established after World War I; it more than tripled in size after World War II; and it grew again, though not nearly as spectacularly, after the Korean conflict. Measures now before Congress would authorize further expansion associated with the Vietnam War. It is important that current proposals be considered carefully in terms of the questions raised here and should not, as seems frequently to be the case, be weighed solely in terms of the merits of showing appreciation for those who have borne arms in their country's defense. There are ways to express such appreciation without involving government in the operation of hospitals or in the administration of medical care.

The VA medical program was established originally to provide hospital care for war veterans suffering from wounds and injuries received, or from illnesses contracted, during their military service. In the mid-1920s, hospital care was also extended, when space was available, to "medically indigent" veterans for conditions which had no "service connection." Outpatient care was made available only to those who had previously been hospitalized. More recently, there has been a trend toward extending the scope of services ranging from dentistry to drug-dependence treatment offered by VA facilities.

The training of health and medical manpower is also perceived as an objective of the VA medical program. Beginning in 1946 and moving rapidly during the past decade, the Veterans Administration has sought to establish close ties between its hospitals and medical schools across the country. This was done primarily as a way to support medical research and to upgrade the quality of the care offered in VA hospitals. The latest development has been the funding of an active role by the Veterans Administration in medical education itself. Concern in Congress for apparent "shortages" of physicians and other health professionals resulted in passage of the Veterans Administration Health Manpower Training Act of 1972. This act directs the Veterans Administration to utilize its hospitals and other health facilities "to the fullest extent" to train physicians, dentists, nurses, and other health professionals, as well as to establish new schools for such training. The act also provides that this activity be funded as a separate item so that resources will not be withdrawn from appropriations intended for the care of patients.

In general, then, the VA medical program has three functions today. It makes medical care available to veterans who qualify, it supports medical research, and it engages in the training of medical and other health manpower.

The Veterans Administration Hospital System

While the Veterans Administration provides only a small portion of this nation's total hospital capacity, the system is large in terms of absolute size. As of the end of fiscal year 1972 it operated 167 widely dispersed hospitals, at least one general hospital in every state with the exception of Alaska and Hawaii. For that same fiscal year, the total operating costs of the VA medical care system exceeded $2.3 billion,[1] almost one million patients were treated, and the average daily census of patients in hospitals and other VA health centers was nearly 114,000.

In addition to general hospitals, the Veterans Administration provides a range of special facilities to serve the medical needs of veterans who do not require hospitalization. Among these facilities are seventy-seven nursing homes containing a total of 5,819 beds. Approximately one-third (8,586) of all VA nursing home patients were treated in these facilities in 1972. The remainder (14,789) received nursing home care in one of the 3,400 private, community nursing homes with which the Veterans Administration has contracts. Patients with non-service-connected disabilities are limited to a maximum of six months of such contract nursing-home care. This accounts at least in part for the higher turnover rate of patients in private homes, which is more than twice that for VA facilities. Another contributing factor is the tendency for more seriously ill patients to remain in VA nursing homes.

The Veterans Administration also operates eighteen facilities which it calls "domiciliaries." These are units serving elderly and disabled veterans who require therapy, training, or rehabilitation, but who do not need hospitalization or skilled nursing care. Nearly 24,000 patients were treated in domiciliaries during the fiscal year 1972. Another 2,444 were treated in restoration centers.

In addition, the Veterans Administration contracts with individual states for the placement of veterans in state homes. Thirty-eight state homes are providing care for more than 25,000 patients under this arrangement. Other facilities include three blind-rehabilitation centers and fourteen spinal-cord injury centers. The former treated 270 patients in fiscal year 1972 and the latter treated a total of 1,466.

Methodological Problems

To assess the performance of such a vast and diverse enterprise, two factors must be considered simultaneously—the cost of production and the nature of the product produced. In the case of the Veterans Administration, neither factor lends itself to ready comparison with analogous data for other hospitals or systems. The costs for VA hospitals, for example, are measured differently from those for private hospitals. The VA hospitals differ organizationally from both voluntary (nonprofit) and proprietary hospitals in that VA staff physicians are largely salaried employees whose salaries are reflected in the hospital cost figures. In contrast, physicians associated with hospitals in the private sector have no financial connection with

3

these hospitals. They bill their patients directly and these costs are not reflected in private hospital cost data. Thus VA hospital costs reflect a different product—hospitalization plus physician services—from private hospital costs and appear to be higher because of this.

Another important difference is in the treatment of capital expenditures. Proprietary hospitals use conventional accounting amortization procedures to cost out the use of capital equipment, buildings, and so forth over the life of these assets. Voluntary hospitals are rather haphazard in their capital cost accounting since they are under less pressure to produce financial statements which accurately reflect their fiscal positions. VA hospitals, on the other hand, are under Office of Management and Budget directive not to include in their costs expenditures for land, buildings or capital equipment. VA reported costs are expected to be lower for this reason.

It is also true that the patient populations of VA and private hospitals are quite different. The VA hospitals have a standard for eligibility which ensures a non-typical patient load. Except during wartime when the wounded and diseased are discharged directly to VA hospitals, not many young people qualify for admission to these facilities. Few of the short-term surgical or medical procedures required by patients populating most private general hospitals result from conditions classifiable as "service-connected," and seldom will a young person demanding such services qualify as "medically indigent." The average age of veterans discharged from VA hospitals was 51.4 years in fiscal year 1972 and has been falling slowly but steadily in recent years from the 1968 figure of 53.1.[2]

Examination of the patient load by type of patient and age is similarly revealing, showing that long-term illness is heavily represented in the VA figures. Only two out of five patients (41 percent) are recorded as being general medical or surgical, the remainder falling into one of the various categories of long-term care. Table 1 shows the breakdown of patients by age in each illness category.

A comparison of the average costs per patient day (called the "per diem" costs), a customary unit of analysis in the study of hospitals, would show variation even if accounting practices were identical. One would expect per diem costs to be lower for the VA patient population than for patients of the typical voluntary general hospital because the latter provides a higher proportion of emergency and short-term care. The requirements of manpower and capital equipment are typically greater for short-term patients than for chronic and longer-term patients.

Finally, questions must be raised regarding the comparative quality of treatment for similar disease conditions. Even if one

Table 1

VA HOSPITALS: PATIENT CENSUS BY AGE AND TYPE,
20 OCTOBER 1971

| Age Group | All Patients | Tuberculous | Psychological | | Neuro-logical | General Medicine & Surgery |
			Psychotic	Other		
Under 25	3,479	22	1,064	847	338	1,208
25-34	5,339	47	2,384	1,113	432	1,363
35-44	10,498	171	4,444	1,946	900	3,037
45-54	24,801	710	8,421	4,101	1,941	9,628
55-64	16,831	491	4,272	2,301	1,420	8,347
65 and over	30,002	298	5,643	2,741	1,845	9,675
Total	81,150	1,689	26,228	13,049	6,926	33,258

Source: U.S. Veterans Administration, *Annual Report 1972, Administrator of Veterans Affairs* (Washington, D.C.: U.S. Government Printing Office, 1973), p. 111.

ignores all of the problems already mentioned of comparing the performance of VA and voluntary hospitals, serious doubt attaches to any comparison focused on costs alone. The costs of caring for patients with particular disabilities may always be reduced by lowering the quality of the care administered. By hiring fewer nurses and physicians and employing paramedical personnel in their places, by crowding patients into wards, by offering fewer ancillary services, and by using old, poorly heated, and un-air-conditioned premises, the average cost per patient may be reduced. This does not imply, of course, that by exploiting all such "economies," one is providing care more efficiently. One is simply providing a different product.

With any product, it requires subtlety to distinguish between inefficiencies in production and quality differences in products. Where two products are traded in the same market at the same price, we may assume with some confidence that they are of equal quality. No one would knowingly pay the same price for a lower quality item. However, when one wishes to compare the quality of two products, one of which is sold to anyone who will buy and the other offered free to a circumscribed set of people, such judgments are virtually impossible to make. We can observe that those individuals to whom the product is offered prefer the item which is available free. What we do *not* know is whether they would be willing to pay a price equal to that of the alternative item, should the price rise from zero to that level. The quality of the free item may be lower, but as long as it is given away, we have no way of assessing this quality directly.[3]

Nor is it clear that the Veterans Administration is concerned, *or should be concerned,* to offer hospital care of identical quality to that offered in the private sector. Arguments have been put forward by economists to the effect that the quality of hospital care available from non-profit voluntary hospitals in the private sector may indeed be "too high," (that is, that such care exhibits attributes which are not worth their cost to buyers or recipients of it).[4] These arguments will be discussed in Chapter II. Here we need only observe that many of the components of modern hospital care have, at best, a tenuous connection with matters of patient health. Such features as television, carpets, telephones and gourmet meals, as well as frequent inquiries and reassurances from the attending staff, may contribute little to the remission of disease, but they are becoming standard in modern hospitals. Other items such as costly and infrequently used radiological equipment may add to the prestige and the cost of a hospital without affecting the hospital's productivity in routine diagnostic or surgical procedures.

It may be the VA's intention to economize on services which do not directly affect health. One might, indeed, expect this to be the case, given reasonable assumptions regarding the incentive structure of VA hospital administrators. This problem is discussed in Chapter III. The point here is simply that administrators of different types of hospitals have considerable discretion in this area. Good reasons may exist for VA administrators to produce a product for consumption by veterans which differs from that available in voluntary and private hospitals.

To sum up, direct comparisons of the cost of producing a patient-day of care by the Veterans Administration and by other hospitals are not very informative. Accounting practices are different and the products are quite different. Whereas in voluntary hospitals the product consists of hospitalization alone, in the VA hospitals it consists of both hospitalization and physician services. Voluntary hospitals contain a high percentage of short-term, high-turnover patients, whereas the Veterans Administration treats a higher percentage of chronic and long-term cases. Finally, the Veterans Administration may choose not to provide some ancillary services which, although provided by voluntary hospitals, are not directly related to the actual health care of patients.

The observation that costs per patient-day for VA hospitals are less than those for voluntary hospitals does not necessarily mean that VA hospitals are more efficient. It may simply reflect the fact that VA hospitals treat less costly cases and do their accounting differently. It may also reflect a lower quality of hospital care.

It is important to distinguish between differences in *quality* and differences in *efficiency*. The level of quality is an independent variable whose value must be explicitly chosen by the providers of care: they can choose to give it a high value or a low one. The costs of producing a particular chosen level of *quality* may vary, however, according to the *efficiency* of production which is applied. Efficiency can only be measured properly when quantities of hospitalization *of constant quality* are being compared. In the absence of market tests of quality, such comparisons of efficiency are impossible to perform.

Cost Comparisons

With this lengthy caveat, we may consider the costs of medical care provided by the Veterans Administration and the costs of that available elsewhere. The Veterans Administration spent a total of $2.4 billion on medical care and research in 1972 and another $107 million on construction. As Table 2 shows, VA spending rose by almost one-and-a-half times in the 1963–73 period, for an annual growth rate of 8.8 percent. Expenditure per patient treated rose at an annual rate of 5.7 percent which compares favorably with changes in medical care prices. During the same decade the hospital price

Table 2

VA EXPENDITURE ON MEDICAL CARE AND RESEARCH
PER PATIENT, AND HOSPITAL PER DIEM COSTS: 1963–73

Fiscal Year	Spending (millions)	Patients Treated (thousands)	Expenditure per Patient Treated	Total Hospital Cost Per Diem
1973	$2,610	1,082	$2,412	$59.25
1972	2,360	944	2,500	53.76
1971	1,997	912	2,190	44.92
1970	1,765	879	2,008	39.69
1969	1,528	868	1,760	32.92
1968	1,430	854	1,674	29.10
1967	1,339	846	1,583	26.48
1966	1,241	825	1,504	24.90
1965	1,195	805	1,484	23.75
1964	1,134	817	1,388	22.43
1963	1,087	794	1,369	21.56

Source: Calculated from U.S. Veterans Administration, *Annual Report 1972, Administrator of Veterans Affairs*, p. 165; U.S. Veterans Administration, *Budget in Brief: Fiscal Year 1975*, p. 77, and VA records.

component of the consumer price index rose at a rate of 10 percent per year, and physician fees increased at 5 percent per year. VA hospital cost per patient day (per diem) registered an annual rate of inflation of 10.1 percent.

In absolute terms, VA costs appear lower than those of private hospitals in some cases and higher in others. The cost of VA general hospitalization compares favorably with private hospital costs. During the fiscal year 1972, these VA costs averaged out at $47.67 per diem for psychiatric-bed sections, $76.48 for surgical-bed sections, and $62.38 for medical-bed sections.[5] This represented a general average cost per diem of $63.73 for all VA general hospitals, compared with the average cost per day for proprietary short-term hospitals of $98.57 during the same period.[6]

The costs being compared are essentially those of different products for the reasons already mentioned. I have attempted to make them commensurable through the following adjustments. Proprietary per diem costs may be represented as

$$\frac{\text{Operating cost} + \text{depreciation}}{\text{Total patient days}},$$

while VA per diem costs are represented as

$$\frac{\text{Operating costs} + \text{physician costs}}{\text{Total patient days}}.$$

VA hospital per diem costs may be made comparable with proprietary per diem costs by adding the following amount to reported VA per diem costs:

$$\frac{\text{Depreciation} - \text{physician costs}}{\text{Total patient days}}.$$

This has been done in Table 3.

Depreciation costs were estimated as follows. It was assumed that the depreciation cost in VA and proprietary hospitals was the same. Depreciation rates were calculated from published financial data for a sample of ten proprietary hospital corporations. These were then multiplied by the total capital stock of proprietary hospitals to obtain an annual depreciation cost. Finally this was divided by the total patient days of care delivered to obtain depreciation costs per patient day. Physician costs were estimated by calculating the total physician wage bill from published data on full-time equivalent physicians employed by the Veterans Administration during the indicated years and salary information supplied by the VA comptroller.

Table 3
VA AND PROPRIETARY HOSPITAL PER DIEM COSTS: 1969–1973

	Veterans Administration				
Year	Reported[a]	Depreciation	MD cost	Net per diem	**Proprietary**
1969	$38.51	$ 6.39	$12.29[b]	$32.61	$ 64.66
1970	46.44	8.97	12.91	42.50	76.80
1971	52.56	11.84	15.35[b]	49.05	87.25
1972	64.23	16.97	17.79	63.41	98.57
1973	69.32	25.44	20.23[b]	74.53	108.31

[a] Standard deviation in reported VA hospital costs in 1968 computed to be $10.60 in 1968. Variance in other years unavailable. Reported costs are for medical and surgical bed sections and exclude costs of psychiatric care.

[b] Interpolated.

Source: American Hospital Association, *Hospitals: Guide Issues 1969–1973;* U.S. House of Representatives, Committee on Veterans Affairs, *Operations of Veterans Administration Hospital and Medical Program;* Standard and Poor's Corporation Records, various years; Veterans Administration records; and the author's computations.

The effect of these adjustments is roughly offsetting as can be seen in Table 3. Proprietary hospital costs remain from 30 to 100 percent higher than VA costs.

Cost comparisons of VA-operated and private community nursing homes may also prove informative. The seventy-seven VA-operated nursing home units contained 5,763 beds as of 30 June 1972 and averaged a daily census during fiscal year 1972 of 5,440 patients. During the same period, the average daily census of VA patients in community nursing homes was 3,990. Although typically the VA provision of private community nursing home care was limited to patients with service-connected illnesses, there appears to be little reason to think that the nature of the care provided differed dramatically from that provided in government-operated homes.

Some selectivity may be practiced by private nursing homes attempting to choose the lowest-cost patients. However, nursing home care is, for the most part, convalescent, regardless of the original cause of hospitalization. Wide variation in costs per diem among different patients should not be observed. We may be confident, furthermore, that the Veterans Administration monitors the services provided by these community nursing homes to ensure that the quality of care is not inferior to that provided in the VA-operated nursing homes.

Finally, the accounting anomalies which interfere with comparisons of costs reported by private and VA general hospitals provide, in the case of nursing homes at least, a *predictable* bias. Physician care costs are included in reported totals for both groups of homes, while capital costs are not included in the costs reported by the VA nursing homes. Nor do the costs reported by the VA homes include the costs of the use of government-owned real estate, buildings, and equipment. Payments made to contract community nursing homes, on the other hand, represent the *full* cost to the government of providing care through this channel. Therefore, comparisons of these costs will show a bias in favor of the VA-operated nursing homes.

Table 4 gives average costs per patient day for nursing home care in VA-operated and in contract community nursing homes. As is apparent, it costs the government considerably more to provide this care directly than to obtain it on a contract basis. According

Table 4
COMPARISON OF PER DIEM COSTS OF VA-OPERATED AND CONTRACT COMMUNITY NURSING HOMES, FISCAL YEAR 1972

	VA-operated	Community
All homes	$29.40	$16.18
American Lake, Washington	21.84	15.23
Bedford, Massachusetts	27.73	16.08
Brockton, Massachusetts	23.49	15.57
Cheyenne, Wyoming	35.76	13.98
Danville, Illinois	25.02	15.89
Fargo, North Dakota	31.95	14.96
Grand Island, Nebraska	44.29	15.26
Levenworth, Kansas	27.23	13.96
Los Angeles, California	31.75	17.36
Montrose, New York	27.11	18.45
Pittsburgh, Pennsylvania	34.67	16.35
Salem, Virginia	29.04	16.83
Sioux Falls, South Dakota	32.88	14.43
Topeka, Kansas	23.32	14.68
Wood, Wisconsin	29.93	17.70
Average of geographically paired samples	29.73	15.78

Source: House of Representatives, Committee on Veterans Affairs, *Veterans Administration Summary of Medical Program—Preliminary, June 1972.*

to these figures, the government could contract for 183 patient days of care from community nursing homes for every 100 that it provides itself. And this comparison, it must be remembered, is biased unrealistically *in favor* of the VA-operated homes.

A comparison of the costs of nursing homes in different parts of the country might, of course, reflect regional differences in wage and other costs rather than the relative efficiency with which care is provided. For example, if all contract community nursing homes were located in the South and if all VA-operated nursing homes were located in the North or Far West, one might expect the costs of community nursing home care to be lower because wages are lower in the South. The same may be said for urban versus rural distributions of the two types of service.

The remainder of Table 4 represents the attempt to eliminate any such regional bias by comparing the costs of VA-operated care and contract community care in the same regions. The average per diem cost of this sample for each category is almost identical to the average for the entire population, indicating that none of the differences in costs is attributable to regional variation. It simply costs more for the Veterans Administration to provide its own nursing home care than it does for it to contract for this service, no matter what part of the country is involved.

Perhaps the most remarkable feature of the individual figures reported is the high variation in the per diem cost among VA-operated nursing homes, and the comparative uniformity of cost for community nursing homes. Per diem costs of VA-operated homes range from $18 to $44, giving a standard deviation of $5.33. The standard deviation for the sample of community nursing homes is only $1.36. The coefficient of variation (which is the standard deviation expressed as a percentage of the mean) for the Veterans Administration figure is 18.1 percent, whereas that for the community nursing homes is only 8.6 percent.

There appears to be no ready technical explanation for this extreme variance in per diem costs of VA-operated nursing homes. Neither size, geographical region, nor turnover rate explain significant portions of this variation. One may interpret the higher level and greater variation in costs to be the result of the noncompetitive environment in which VA nursing homes operate. Indeed, both observations are consistent with such an interpretation. More uniform prices and lower costs for marketed output are implied by economic theories of non-market and bureaucratic behavior. Discussion of such implications will be deferred to Chapters II and III of this study.

The Cost of Well-Being

Disregarding the ambiguities discussed earlier concerning cost comparisons between different institutions, the cost per patient day of hospitalization considers only one dimension of efficiency. Resources could be combined in order to provide a particular quality of hospital care at absolutely minimum cost, and yet resources could still be wasted.

Hospitalization is, after all, an intermediate good used in the production of physical well-being. It must be combined with many other inputs to produce the final product, and the combining may be done either wastefully or efficiently. If, for example, patients are retained in hospitals when they might be treated just as well in nursing homes or as outpatients, then resources are being wasted. The hospital, because it is complex and costly, should be reserved for patients who need the full range of expert services and exotic equipment found there. If patients who do have legitimate problems requiring hospital treatment or surgery are admitted to hospitals but experience lengthy delays before receiving treatment, then the patients' time as well as the hospitals' resources are being wasted.

Considerable evidence exists that VA hospitals are not free of this sort of waste. The criticism most frequently leveled at VA hospital operations is that many patients occupying space in these hospitals have no medical condition warranting hospitalization. Some patients are admitted for care which might be administered effectively to them as outpatients. Others are admitted for tests or surgery which, because of scheduling problems or other difficulties, cannot be performed for several days. For a variety of reasons, some patients apparently are retained in hospitals when they might be released to nursing homes or treated as outpatients. The net result of this is that hospital capacity is poorly utilized.

Mr. Dudley Porter of the Health Insurance Association of America, in testimony before a congressional subcommittee investigating hospital personnel needs, reported his finding that average lengths of stay for patients hospitalized in VA hospitals were longer than those for patients undergoing the same surgical procedures in private hospitals.[7] Similar findings are shown in Table 5 (which appears in Chapter 3). The hypothesis of excessive lengths of stay in the VA hospitals is supported by these results.

Dr. S. Richardson Hill, director of the Medical Center of the University of Alabama and a member of the medical staff of the VA hospital in Birmingham, told a Senate subcommittee that "because of delays in obtaining tests, such as GI series, glucose tolerance tests, and other tests which they feel are procedurally necessary to diagnose and treat their patients, . . . sometimes the patient has to remain in the hospital 2 or 3 weeks longer than he would otherwise, just to get a particular test." [8] Testifying before the same subcommittee was Dr. Philip R. Lee, chancellor of the University of California, San Francisco, a medical school. At the request of a member of this subcommittee, Dr. Lee provided the following statement for the record:

> In San Francisco there are 22 non-Federal hospitals which provide care for patients with acute medical and surgical conditions. The average length of stay in these hospitals for the period July 1, 1970 to December 31, 1970 was 8 days. During this same period at the San Francisco Veterans Administration Hospital, which also provides care for veterans with acute medical and surgical conditions, the average length of stay was 19 days. [9]

Dr. Lee and Dr. Hill both indicated that these delays in treatment and prolonged stays are attributable to inadequate financing, particularly with regard to personnel. Indeed, a recurrent theme in the testimony at this hearing was the injustice and inefficiency brought about by the Office of Management and Budget when it delayed the expenditure of $105 million appropriated by Congress in excess of the President's budget and subsequently applied roughly one-third of this amount to fund unbudgeted pay-raise costs. Closer examination reveals, however, that the problems which generate prolonged stays are varied, and are not necessarily of the sort that can be eliminated by the infusion of more money.

The Quality of VA Care

Before turning to discussions of hypotheses which attempt to explain the behavior and problems of the VA medical system, however, let us consider the evidence regarding another dimension of VA hospital performance, namely, the *quality* of the care provided. In recent years hospitals and other medical institutions operated by the Veterans Administration have been the subject of criticism regarding the care and environment provided to their patients. These allegations have been made by personnel within the VA medical care system as well as by the press and other outside observers.

Foremost among these complaints is the frequently lamented "shortage" of personnel, particularly of staff physicians and nurses. A questionnaire prepared by the Committee on Veterans' Affairs requested individual hospitals in the VA system to list their most pressing needs. Of the roughly 160 hospitals responding to this inquiry, more than 100 mentioned staffing as their primary problem.[10] It is clear that administrators of these hospitals feel that present staffing levels are too low to provide the desired level of care and comfort. It is also apparent that staff levels in VA hospitals are considerably below those found in community nonfederal hospitals. The overall staff/patient ratio for all hospitals of the Veterans Administration is 1.3:1.[11] Veterans Administration standards require staff/patient ratios of 1:1 for psychiatric hospitals and 2:1 for general acute hospitals. Actual ratios reported in 1970 were 0.94:1 for psychiatric hospitals and 1.5:1 for general hospitals.[12] During the same year voluntary community hospitals had an average staff/patient ratio of 2.9:1.[13] Merely to bring staff levels up to the adjusted minimum standards set by the Veterans Administration itself would require the addition of 25,659 staff members to the psychiatric and general hospitals combined.[14] Better scheduling to reduce the patient census would, of course, improve this ratio without increasing the staff.

A comparison of staff levels tells us as little about the quality of medical care provided by hospitals as cost comparisons tell us about efficiency. If staff distribution is inefficient, or if the staff is inattentive or unqualified, then high staff/patient ratios may not reflect high quality care. Objective measures of quality are crude. Further, as was mentioned earlier, quality as defined in terms of the objectives of the federal government and the Veterans Administration may be quite different from the concept of quality held by the staff of university hospitals.

Nevertheless, evidence which has come to light in recent years has been interpreted by the press and by members of Congress as examples of gross defects in the VA hospital system. No discussion of the quality of care provided by the Veterans Administration can be considered complete without a thorough review of this evidence and the incidents which brought it to light.

The first incident was the 1970 appearance before the Senate Subcommittee on Veterans' Affairs of Dr. Gary Davidson and Dr. Bernhard Votteri, senior medical residents at Wadsworth Veterans Administration Hospital in Los Angeles. These doctors brought with them more than forty sworn affidavits attesting to the deficiencies and inadequacies of the care provided at that hospital, together with photographs depicting, among other things, crowded offices, halls, and wards, a leaky roof, dirty windows, and unwashed dishes. The charges made by these physicians extended far beyond simple crowding and untidiness, however. They stated that lives were being lost

14

which might have been saved had financing been made available for more equipment and staff.[15] Among supporting affidavits presented to the committee were references to two specific deaths and one near-death attributable to the failure or non-availability of standard hospital ward equipment.[16] Three deaths and one near-death were alleged to have resulted from inadequate nursing.[17] Among this latter group was an affidavit of a resident, Raul Guisado, M.D., reporting an incident involving a Vietnam veteran twenty-one years of age. A tracheostomy had been performed on this patient to facilitate ventilation and clearing of secretions. According to Dr. Guisado, "[B]ecause of lack of [an] intensive care unit and available special nursing care, inadequate and infrequent tracheal suctioning was provided. Moreover, on one occasion the patient's mother was compelled to suction the tracheostomy stoma, having recognized an existing exigency." [18]

Returning to testify before the subcommittee the following year, these doctors, together with Dr. John Messenger, acting director of the coronary care unit at Wadsworth VA Hospital, presented additional evidence of neglect at this hospital. They reported that in spite of their protestations the previous year, only ten nurses had been added to the staff. Three additional deaths and several near-deaths were reported to have resulted from inadequate nursing and lack of equipment.[19]

The statements of these physicians regarding conditions in the Wadsworth hospital were widely reported in the press. Newspapers and other sources soon published accounts of similar deficiencies in other Veterans Administration hospitals. Senator Alan Cranston used a May 1971 series of *Miami Herald* articles as an appendix to his statement before the Appropriations Committee requesting an additional $391 million for the Veterans Administration. Senator Cranston also appended to this statement several of the affidavits presented at earlier hearings over which he had presided. Among those affidavits was the following memorandum signed by a junior medical resident of Wadsworth Hospital.

> Mr. Arthur Ford was admitted to Wadsworth on 12/13/71 with a diagnosis of chronic renal failure which was fairly well compensated with diet and koyexalate. While awaiting indefinitely for placement into an extended nursing care situation and because of the nursing shortage on this ward, the patient was not given adequate oral fluids and died from dehydration aggravating his renal diseases. It is intolerable that someone should die because of a lack of personnel to give an occasional glass of water.[20]

The incident most damaging to the Veterans Administration's reputation as a provider of hospital services, however, was a *Life* cover story, "From Vietnam to a VA Hospital: Assignment to Neglect," published 22 May 1970. Focusing attention on the Bronx VA Hospital and on patients of its spinal cord injury center, this article labeled the VA hospital "a medical slum" and described conditions as "medieval" and "filthy." It depicted a paralyzed patient left for some time in a shower waiting to be dried, other paralyzed patients waiting unattended for up to four hours for treatment, a dead mouse in a trap by a patient's bed, and overflowing garbage cans next to occupied beds.

The image of VA hospitals created by unfavorable press coverage and congressional testimony probably has remained the popular image. Senator Cranston, for example, has stated that he considers these reports to be "accurate." [21] Continued demonstrations of dissatisfaction among veterans eventually forced the resignation of VA Administrator Donald E. Johnson in 1974. During his tenure, however, Administrator Johnson consistently maintained that medical care provided by the VA hospital system was "second to none." The publicity which attended the charges of negligence and mismanagement unfortunately has not been followed by equivalent coverage of the reports of audit teams and investigations which found most of these charges exaggerated or groundless.

In response to the original charges brought before the Senate subcommittee, a special Central Office task force was dispatched to look into the allegations pertaining to conditions at Wadsworth Hospital in Los Angeles. The report of the task force recognized limitations imposed by an outmoded physical plant and a shortage of personnel, but it concluded, "Patient care is professionally of high quality, with emphasis being placed on rapid and proper diagnosis and vigorous, sophisticated therapy." Unfortunately, although members of the press and television crews accompanied the task force on its investigatory tour, few of the results of the investigation found their way into publication or other news coverage. Later investigating teams also presented a picture of care provided at Wadsworth and other VA hospitals that differed radically from that described at the Senate hearings. In a letter to Senator Cranston apprising him of the findings of this team, Administrator Johnson reported:

> Our auditors reviewed the records of a total of nine patients whose cases had been cited . . . as possible examples of patient deaths attributable to alleged deficiencies about which [Votteri, Davidson, *et al.*] testified.

Our audit team carefully explored each case, examining hospital records including doctors' orders and progress notes, nurses' progress notes, consultation reports, autopsy protocols, and other pertinent records to determine the extent of the treatment provided and the recorded cause of death. They interviewed the available professional staff members who had worked on each case. The resulting data were analyzed in detail by physicians in our Department of Medicine and Surgery, VA Central Office. Summaries of these cases are enclosed. The evidence developed in these cases does not substantiate the allegations that the proximate cause of these deaths was the result of the hospital not having adequate staff or equipment.[22]

Appended to the letter were summaries of the findings of the investigating team. Each of the allegations as reported to the audit team was listed together with the team's findings regarding that case. In none of the cases was there support for the allegation that death was due to lack of equipment or inadequate nursing. In several cases, patients had died in spite of special nursing procedures that were ordered and provided "promptly and in optimal fashion." In the one documented case of equipment failure associated with a patient's death, records indicated that "backup systems were available for emergencies and were used in this patient's treatment." According to the auditors, this particular equipment irregularity did not contribute to the patient's death.

Regarding the case in which the patient allegedly died because there was a "lack of personnel to give an occasional glass of water," it was concluded that "there was no indication either from the nursing or progress notes that this patient received inadequate amounts of fluid from neglect of the nurses."

The reports of several investigating teams present a radically different picture of care provided at VA hospitals from that described before the Senate subcommittees. Charges of neglectful and deficient care arising from shortages of staff and equipment were not substantiated. These investigators' reports convey a picture of a conscientious and dedicated staff that is hampered by an old 'but serviceable hospital environment but is providing care of good quality to more patients than the facilities were designed to handle. Such a situation can be frustrating, particularly to young physicians fresh from internship in a teaching hospital, whose equipment and staff are supported as part of the educational program.

The charges leveled at Wadsworth seem to have been unfounded; the accusations made in the *Life* exposé of the Bronx Spinal Cord Injury Center remain to be examined here. Publication of this article, with its morbid pictures of what was alleged to be typical treatment of patients there, brought an immediate reaction from Administrator Johnson and other spokesmen for the Veterans Administration. Dr. A. M. Kleinman, director of the Bronx VA Hospital, responded with a letter to the editor of *Life* in which he charged that the pictures contained in the article had been "posed to illustrate a point." The points illustrated, according to Kleinman, were either "untruthful . . . or a partial or distorted truth."

Among the charges made by Dr. Kleinman were (1) that a picture of a patient in a shower stall "waiting helplessly to be dried" was actually taken after an assistant who had been soaping the patient "was asked to step aside by the photographer who wished to take this picture." (2) That patients depicted as waiting "up to four hours to be attended by a single aide" had in fact all been administered enemas and were experiencing the normal wait (for paralyzed patients) of several hours for evacuation to be completed. (3) That the picture allegedly showing a patient lying naked and neglected in "a partitionless ward" surrounded by a "disarray of dirty linen" was also posed. Cubicle curtains, normally drawn when patients are cared for, were pulled out of sight "at the direction of the photographer." The dirty linen revealed in the photograph was a sheet which had been used to cover the patient as he was wheeled back from the shower (immediately prior to the taking of the photograph) and clean pillows used to position the patient's body. Another patient shown asleep in the same picture stated that he bitterly resented being photographed without his knowledge or consent and would have refused to give permission had he been asked. This patient "feels that the Bronx VA saved his life, and is thankful for the care which he receives. . . ." (4) The presence of mice in the hospital was acknowledged, though the presence of rats was denied by experts consulted. (5) Trash cans shown in close proximity to patients in the enema room were pushed from their normal location behind a curtain "toward the patient for misleading photographic effect." [23]

An investigation of *Life*'s charges was instituted which consisted of interviews with ten employees and six patients who were involved in or witnessed the photography in progress. Its findings support in detail the charges made by Dr. Kleinman. Based on these interviews the investigators conclude that "some of the photographs were staged by the *Life* magazine representatives and that the photograph captions are false or misleading." On three occasions during one photographic session, August Gomez, a nursing assistant, was asked to step out of range, apparently so that the patient's seeming isolation might reinforce the impression of neglect. Four of the six patients interviewed stated that the picture of conditions at the Bronx VA Hospital depicted by the *Life* article was inaccurate.[24]

The purpose of reviewing these incidents in such detail has been to attempt to give a broader perspective to events which are to a considerable extent responsible for the unfavorable reputation which Veterans Administration hospitals currently enjoy. It is apparent that reports of satisfied and grateful patients, selfless dedication and service, economical administration, and skillful medicine are unlikely to generate much excitement among members of Congress or the press. On the other hand, a hint of scandal attracts immediate attention regardless of whether the allegations are true or false.

By objective standards, medical care provided by Veterans Administration hospitals appears to be of good quality. Not one of the 167 hospitals in the system has failed to receive accreditation by the Joint Commission on Hospital Accreditation. Admittedly many of the facilities are old, inconvenient, and difficult to maintain. In comparison to the sparkling new facilities springing up across the country that have been financed through the Medicare-Medicaid programs, the VA system is clearly "taking a back seat" with regard to federal health care dollars. Nevertheless, the Veterans Administration has continued to deliver care that is not demonstrably inferior in a therapeutic sense to that provided through other health care delivery institutions in the United States. Though evidence has been offered that VA hospitals utilize less manpower per patient than other hospitals do, detractors have failed to establish that this impairs the ability of these hospitals to care for patients.

CHAPTER II

PRIVATE HOSPITALS FOR PROFIT AND NOT FOR PROFIT

The performance of VA hospitals may not be judged without reference to other types of hospitals. Furthermore, even if cost data for VA and private hospitals could be made perfectly commensurable and the qualities and quantities of outputs produced were identical, the interpretation of the results would remain ambiguous. For example, consider a hypothetical finding under these controlled circumstances which indicated that, on average, VA hospitals operated at higher cost than did hospitals in the private sector during the period of study. Would we interpret this to imply (1) that veterans make demanding and costly patients, (2) that the administrator of Veterans Affairs was an ineffective executive, (3) that the format of the VA health care delivery system itself promotes waste, or (4) that government hospitals as such cannot be expected to operate as efficiently as hospitals in the private sector? Cost comparisons alone do not permit discrimination among these alternative explanations.

In order to attempt some identification of the nature of the differences in the behavior of VA and other types of hospitals, we must examine models of these alternative institutions. Empirically verified models may then be compared, and inferences concerning such differences may be drawn from the models themselves. The results of such an approach will ultimately prove more informative and provide more insights into variations in behavior than arid statistical comparisons of alternative sets of data.

There are three basic organizational forms for delivery of hospital services. By far the most significant of these from the standpoint of numbers of hospitals or hospital beds is the *voluntary* hospital. Voluntary hospitals are nominally in the private sector; they are owned by private individuals or organizations. The distinguishing characteristic of voluntary hospitals is that they are not operated for profit. Generally they are sponsored by churches or charitable organizations and placed under the control of appointed boards of trustees who are instructed to price the medical care provided at the level necessary to "cover costs."

Second most significant as an organizational form are *government-operated* hospitals. These hospitals are owned and operated by some branch of government in the United States. Included in this group, in addition to Veterans Administration hospitals, are military-service hospitals and hospitals operated by states and local governments. A significant number of these are municipal hospitals located in large cities and organized originally to serve the needs of the indigent. Funds for their support are derived principally from the sponsoring government. Fees charged are usually based upon "ability to pay" and are not intended to cover all operating costs.

Smallest in number and admissions, but growing rapidly under the impetus of the large increase in demand resulting from the introduction of Medicare and Medicaid, is the third form of hospital service delivery system, the *proprietary* hospital. These hospitals correspond organizationally to the classic model of the private firm. They are privately owned and financed and operated with the intention of earning profits. Prices are presumably determined by market behavior. Because it provides a convenient point of departure for discussion of the other less familiar and theoretically less tractable forms of organization, the proprietary hospital will be discussed first.

Proprietary Hospitals

A proprietary hospital is organized and operated to earn profits for its owners, as is a bank, a food store, or a textile mill. There are two fundamental processes which influence such firms to produce products which display the qualities and attributes desired by their customers and to supply them at low cost. The first of these is the desire of the existing supplier for profits. As the supplier recognizes that the price he may obtain for a given quantity of the product (of a given quality) is not affected by the cost of producing it, he will wish to produce at lowest cost. In so doing he will maximize the value of the residual left when all costs of production are met. He will also seek to produce, for similar reasons, the quality of product which consumers want. Consumers will be willing to pay more for a product if it exhibits more desired attributes than does a similar product. Profits are maximized by providing the consumer with what he wants.

Private firms are thus led by selfish interest to produce at lowest cost a product which meets the specifications of its purchasers. These firms will seek to avoid the waste of resources that results from organizing their use inefficiently or from providing product attributes not desired, because such waste reduces profits.

Profit maximization within producing firms is not sufficient to ensure that their products are available at prices equal to marginal cost, that is, efficient prices. Output, though efficiently produced, may be restricted and prices kept high. Competition among sellers of the same product will ensure low prices, however. Though individual producers in a market might prefer to keep prices high, outsiders can be counted on to recognize a profitable opportunity for entry. New entrants, attracted by high profits in an industry, will seek to undercut existing sellers and thereby cause all prices to fall.

These two processes, profit maximization and competition, will produce this salutary result under a wide variety of conditions. No benevolence on the part of producers nor interference by government is required to ensure the availability or quality of those products for which individuals are willing to pay the value of resources used in their production. As noted above, however, only a small part of the hospital industry in this country is organized by profit-seeking entrepreneurs. To a large extent, this may be explained by three phenomena: (1) state laws preventing proprietary organization of hospitals, (2) professional regulations enforced by licensing bodies and certifying agencies in the various states, and (3) the availability of large federal capital subsidies through the Hill-Burton program to municipal and nonprofit voluntary hospitals.

Objections to Proprietary Organization. Reasons commonly advanced to justify the suppression of proprietary hospitals are not particularly convincing. One explanation frequently encountered holds that it is unethical to seek to earn a profit from disease or misfortune—that society prefers to respond to such needs through charitable rather than selfish motives. As Kenneth Arrow has pointed out, however, consistency in this attitude would require similar reliance on voluntarism for organization of the pharmaceutical industry and other allied health industries which have traditionally been left to market organization.[1]

A more specific objection to allowing profits to be earned by hospitals has been suggested by Herbert E. Klarman. He notes that privately organized hospitals would result in profits being added to cost, raising the price of hospital care to those who must pay for it: "Furthermore, since nobody derives dividends from a nonprofit hospital, it is postulated that cost of production must be lower than in a similar institution conducted as a business; in other words, the potential contribution of entrepreneurship is neglected." [2] This position manifestly misinterprets the conventional theory of the competitive firm, however. Profit is not added to cost to determine price; it is a residual retained by the owner of the firm after all costs have been met. It exists as a return to entrepreneurship only if there is some entrepreneurship, that is, some cost-reducing innovation by the firm.

Klarman's argument also confuses profits and capital returns. It is clearly true that, to the extent that much of the capital used in voluntary hospitals comes from government grants or private donations, costs may be lower for these hospitals than for proprietary hospitals who must recover in revenues the rental value of such equipment. As long as the price to proprietaries of hospital care is high enough to cover these extra costs, however, it is apparent that such charity as is evidenced by the existence of voluntary hospitals is insufficient to make this advantage important. In other words, if proprietary hospitals can cover their costs at the prices which they confront in this market, then it is clear that there is an inadequate supply of the low-cost subsidized care to satisfy demand at those prices. To deny proprietaries access to this market because they charge higher prices than voluntaries is to deny sick patients hospitalization which they need and for which they are willing to pay.

Another rather narrow argument leveled against proprietaries is that these hospitals typically "skim off the cream" of the hospital market.[3] Analysis of this cream-skimming argument requires a brief statement of the alleged pricing policy of nonprofit hospitals. Voluntaries and municipal hospitals are said to be engaged in *philanthropic pricing*. This practice is said to involve padding the bills for some patients and procedures so that below-cost prices may be charged for other patients and procedures. For example, the price of x-rays is typically inflated to provide a subsidy for more costly and exotic procedures such as cobalt therapy and open heart surgery. Such hospitals also allegedly load the bills of patients who are expected to pay in order to finance the care administered to those who cannot or will not pay. Skimming (that is, competition) on the part of proprietary hospitals involves a bidding away of this business which the nonprofit hospitals price above cost, leaving the latter no choice but to raise the price of their charity work.

Newhouse and Acton [4] have examined this skimming argument from three points of view: First, they question the amount of charity allegedly provided by hospitals. Second, they question the merits of utilizing revenues derived from the treatment of some diseases to subsidize the treatment of other diseases. Third, they question the appropriateness of underwriting the care of nonpayers by loading the fees of patients with higher collection rates.

Regarding the first question, Newhouse and Acton find that the amount of charity extended by hospitals is small and diminishing. Much of this charity was dispensed in the past to those now entitled to government-financed care through Medicare and Medicaid, that is, the elderly and the poor. They report that in 1970 only 1.5 percent of hospital expenditures could be attributed to philanthropy in any form. Clearly we must consider quite soberly the merits of suppressing proprietary hospitals in an effort to protect philanthropic price discrimination practiced to this meager extent.

Newhouse and Acton also question the appropriateness of the cross-procedure subsidy. Such a practice must occasionally involve the transfer of purchasing power from persons with low income who happen to require a profitable treatment to others with higher income needing unprofitable procedures. The transfer of income from the sick poor to the sick rich which occurs under this kind of pricing structure is inconsistent with conventional distributional norms and seems to be a poor justification for opposing proprietary organization. In this connection, Newhouse and Acton note that by pricing treatments in this way (that is, not in proportion to the marginal costs of each procedure) incentives are introduced to "overproduce" unprofitable treatment and "underproduce" profitable treatment. Price distortion and the allocative inefficiencies thus introduced are cited as another reason why such philanthropic pricing is "undesirable."

The third argument questions the merits of subsidizing the treatment of those less likely to pay their bills by padding the bills of better payers. According to Newhouse and Acton, "The reimbursement for bad debts is appropriately made by those who benefit from having bad debtors receive treatment. Since this is more likely to be society as a whole, and not just those who are hospitalized, this argues for reimbursement from general revenues." [5]

Markets with Imperfect Information. A more plausible argument against organization of the hospital industry by profit-seeking firms concerns the cost of assessing the quality of the product produced. For profit maximization to produce the salutary effects suggested earlier, the purchaser must be confident that the product possesses those properties and characteristics claimed for it by the seller. Arrow has argued that the cost of obtaining information about the quality of medical care is prohibitively expensive.[6] Years of training are necessary to evaluate directly the quality of care provided by a hospital or physician. The inspection process is further complicated by the fact that the product often purchased from these suppliers is information, which cannot be evaluated until it is received. The patient may, for example, seek information concerning his projected future well-being and the appropriate course of treatment for an "unidentified" disease associated with a set of symptoms. Until he has obtained the product (the diagnosis), the patient is at a loss to determine its value.

Arrow and others have predicted that market organization under such circumstances will produce inefficiency. Lacking the ability to assess quality, it is argued that demanders will expect profit-maximizing sellers to misrepresent their products and will thus undervalue hospital or medical services supplied. Suppliers, on the other hand, will be unable to convince demanders of the therapeutic content in services and thus will be influenced to under-provide it. Underproduction of medical services is predicted in these circumstances.

Various responses to this problem have been suggested, and coincidentally the solutions offered are not unlike many of the institutions observed in the existing medical care industry. Licensure of medical practitioners to ensure the quality of their services has been explained (that is, justified) in these terms. Nonprofit organization of hospitals likewise has been viewed as a means of reassuring demanders that suppliers of these services are not misrepresenting their quality.

Exponents of this latter view have overlooked alternative means of providing such reassurance and are perhaps overly sanguine regarding the ability of nonprofit organizations to supply it without introducing other serious consequences. As is well known, it is people—not institutions—who are greedy, and the fact that certain institutions are organized in such a way that owners are not residual claimants does not imply that these institutions cannot be used for private gain. Although a fully satisfactory model of voluntary hospital behavior has yet to be developed and validated empirically, this lacuna should not be interpreted as support for the view that such institutions invariably choose to behave in globally optimizing ways. The absence of such a model suggests simply that we do not know what is responsible for the anomalies associated with voluntary hospital organization.

Furthermore, the kinds of uncertainties surrounding the provision of hospital care are far from unique. The assessment of need for mechanical work on an automobile requires ability beyond that possessed by most purchasers. The quality of a restaurant meal or a haircut cannot be stipulated effectively in the contract to purchase. The value of prepackaged foods and other products may in principle be severely depreciated without risking prosecution for fraud. I would suggest that the incidence of customer dissatisfaction is far less frequent than one might predict on the basis of the number of opportunities which exist for such misrepresentation.

One inhibitor of misrepresentation is the host of risk-sharing devices which have emerged in the market in response to buyers' uncertainty. We observe warranties, service contracts, and "money-back guarantees" that allow customers to void transactions in which the good or service obtained does not meet customer expectations. Another effective technique for generating purchaser confidence in the product or service marketed is the establishment of a reputation for honest dealing. Advertising and the creation of a brand name are used by producers as a means of providing quality reassurance to customers.[7]

It is interesting to note that for many years some proprietary hospitals flourished in states in which proprietary hospitals were not explicitly banned but were denied certification by the Joint Commission on Accreditation. Despite assertions made by those committed to nonprofit hospital organization, no evidence has ever demonstrated that care provided in proprietary hospitals is systematically inferior to that provided by hospitals organized differently. Perhaps the danger of misrepresentation would be even less if proprietary hospitals were encouraged to advertise.

There seems, in fact, little reason to expect that misrepresentation would pose a serious problem, were hospitals widely organized for profit. Even if the deterrents to such behavior discussed above were inadequate to eliminate deception, other techniques exist for controlling it than suppressing hospitals organized for profit. Certification or grading of quality, practiced widely by government in agriculture, packaging, and transportation for example, is one method. Licensing or direct regulation are more elaborate and, to a certain extent, more costly ways of ensuring the quality of medical output. The point is that the nonprofit voluntary hospital, almost exclusively relied upon in the post–World War II period to provide hospital services, is not, at least on a priori grounds, a necessary component of an efficient health care delivery system. Were legal and professional barriers to the organization of hospitals for profit eliminated along with the special subsidies which voluntaries enjoy, there is little doubt that proprietaries would dramatically increase in number. Nor do we have reason to expect that the quality of hospital services provided would suffer as a result.

Voluntary Hospitals

While economists agree on many behavioral characteristics of competitive firms (even under conditions of imperfect information) no such consensus exists regarding a model of nonprofit organization behavior. Thus, while we may infer a great many things about the behavior of proprietary hospitals in different settings, we must approach the task of making similar predictions about voluntaries with some apprehension. Although a number of economists have attempted to produce a theory of nonprofit organization, none has yet succeeded in developing one that is fully satisfying.

The fundamental difficulty of these attempts springs from the ambiguity of the objectives to be pursued by nonprofit organizations. The profit-maximizing firm has one objective—to increase the net worth of its owners—and predicting its behavior is simply a matter of rank-ordering behavioral options in terms of this criterion. For example, if an individual is engaged in activity that contributes less to revenues than it costs, then we would expect a profit-seeking firm to release him or at least find him a more suitable job to perform. On the other hand, employing personnel in low-productivity activities may be consistent with the broader objectives of a nonprofit firm.

A nonprofit (or not-for-profit) organization by definition has objectives different from that postulated for the classical profit-seeking firm. In many cases these objectives are unique to a particular organization, multiple and competitive in nature, and generally unspecified except in the vaguest language. Voluntary hospitals, for example, are organized by their sponsors to make hospital services available to the communities they are intended to serve. Because profits are not sought by these hospitals, criteria other than profitability or cost-effectiveness must be established regarding such important decisions as the quantity of services to be supplied, the mix of services to be made available, the quality of each of the services provided, and the pricing scheme to be adopted for the services offered. Vague guidance expressed in terms of a desire to "serve the hospital needs of the community" is inadequate; it simply raises questions regarding the definition of a legitimate need and the priorities to be established among competing needs or requirements.

The Problem of Central Planning and Efficiency. A prevalent belief among health planners and medical economists in this country is that management decisions should be made on the basis of economic efficiency—that economic inefficiency as it exists in the hospital industry should be eliminated. It is argued that unnecessary and wasteful "duplication" of costly and "underutilized" facilities should be curtailed, organizational red tape should be cut, and resource use within the industry should be rationalized. Documentation of waste and inefficiency in the medical service industry has filled many pages of commentary and accounts for the pressures to change organization policy.[8]

Many who have observed the waste in the existing system of voluntary hospitals see the solution of this problem to be regional health planning of hospital resources. They propose to overcome the "random" and "uncoordinated" character of existing hospital facilities by imposing structure and foresight on the system.

The Hill-Burton program, which makes available on a matching basis federal financing for voluntary-hospital construction, provided in the original act of 1946 for development of statewide plans for expansion based on an inventory of existing facilities and "deficiencies." This Hill-Burton machinery has had little real impact on the dispersion of control within the system, however. More recently the Public Health Service has promoted and financed development of local planning groups. Lack of effective enforcement mechanisms has weakened the influence of these bodies, however. Passage of the National Health Planning and Resources Act of 1974 enlists government's power and purse to make planning edicts enforceable.[9]

One may question the unwavering faith placed in central planning by these writers. Few who advance planning as a solution seem to understand what generates the waste which they perceive. Most seem willing to attribute waste simply to the lack of central direction of operations or investment. Anyone who has studied the VA hospital system can deny this naive prescription, however. Central direction and planning within the Veterans Administration has not silenced the identifiers of "discontinuity," "conflicting functions," and "underutilization," the familiar slogans of the hospital planning literature.

After all, many industries in this country seem to operate effectively without central coordination. And those most extensively regulated (for example, transportation) exhibit exactly the sort of waste often attributed to lack of planning (for example, underutilization). As we have noted, under certain circumstances uncoordinated profit-seeking behavior in competitive markets promotes efficient utilization of resources. The appropriate area to explore in this regard would therefore seem to be the differences in objectives of, and constraints confronting, voluntary hospital management and staff, which suggest behavior differing from the competitive model. Information regarding what individuals in such organizations wish to do, and what they are effectively constrained not to do, is more valuable than information we are repeatedly given now—that is, information regarding things which hospitals are *not ordered* to do or not do.

Theories of Nonprofit Organizations. Most studies of voluntary hospitals which adopt this approach assume that management seeks to maximize output or output in combination with some other characteristic, subject to a budget constraint. Joseph Newhouse, in perhaps the best-known attempt to model the voluntary hospital, selects output and quality as the items to be jointly maximized and says these objectives lead to inefficiency for two reasons.[10] First, voluntary hospitals are allegedly biased against offering low-quality hospital services even though fully informed consumers might prefer lower quality (and lower cost!) hospital care. Secondly, Newhouse cites barriers to entry resulting from nonprofit status. These barriers are the result of philanthropy, favorable tax treatment, legal impediments to entry, and the absence of rewards for managerial and entrepreneurial activity.

Elaboration of the first of these reasons seems called for. Quality of hospital care is allegedly valued by management for its prestige value as well as for its therapeutic value. However, because the patient presumably values only the latter but must pay the cost of both, management predictably invests excessive amounts in quality.

Newhouse's theory is based on the assumption that administrators and trustees (to the extent that this group influences management) share this dual quality-quantity objective. The theory is vague regarding why quality per se should be valued by either group, however. Newhouse cites a number of statements attesting to the importance of maintaining the "highest quality," but none of these statements suggests that ethics or good practice demand that quality be higher than patients would be willing to pay for. On the contrary, one of the quotations closes with the statement, "The patient expects that hospital services will be of high quality." [11] Concern for quality hospital care that arises in response to patient willingness to pay for more quality will not result in excessively high quality.

Others, in seeking to model hospital behavior, have sought to retain wealth maximization as the objective of all individuals but to identify changes in the constraint structure across institutional settings as the explanation for behavioral differences. Elsewhere I have attempted to focus on the role played by the medical staff of hospitals in this regard.[12] There it was argued that the medical staff of voluntary hospitals can and do control hospital operations with the objective of maximizing the profits of their own practices.

Medical staff control manifests itself in the following way. Control is exercised over hospital management and investment policy to ensure that hospital services offered are complementary rather than substitutes for their own services. This is particularly important since it appears that medical practitioners may as a group possess excess training.[13] Hence substitute care that was less human-capital-intensive, which a competitive hospital might offer, could seriously diminish demand for physicians. Outpatient and emergency facilities which conceivably could serve as substitutes for staff physician services are predicted to be under-provided, while operating theaters and costly radiological equipment are readily financed.

Fostering this tendency toward apparent over-provision of certain types of hospital capital is the fact that physicians are customarily on the staff of only one or two hospitals in their communities. Lack of equipment for treatment of a particular medical exigency at his particular hospital would mean that a doctor would have to refer all such patients to a physician on the staff of another hospital. If hospital capital were privately financed, competitive forces in this market might still be relied upon to foster the proper amount of specialization among hospitals. Much of the capital supplied to voluntary hospitals is donated, however.[14] The medical staff can be expected to devote such funds to the purchase of equipment as long as it is useful at all, regardless of whether its services are worth the cost.

In a similar but more elaborate model, Pauly and Redisch also use maximization of physicians' income as the voluntary hospital's objective.[15] They extend the theory of the cooperative, developed by Ward, Domar, and Oi and Clayton,[16] to hospital organization. They assume that hospitals are operated by the physician staff so as to maximize equal shares of the residual from operations. It is argued that the behavior of closed-staff hospitals [17] is similar to that predicted for cooperatives regarding response to changes in demand for output or changes in factor prices. Increases in the demand for hospital services may be associated with reductions in output and the number of physicians admitted to the staff. Increases in factor prices, on the other hand, may be associated with expansion of operations by these hospitals. Expected philanthropy leads to a contraction in staff size.

Pauly and Redisch argue that the inelastic supply response of hospitals to Medicare and Medicaid witnessed over the past several years is consistent with their model. They also claim that widely noted "duplication of facilities" is an implication of the closed-staff variation of their model. Inefficient use of resources is also attributed to "imperfect cooperation" by the medical staff, though this part of the paper does not seem to be completely worked out.[18]

Perhaps the most satisfactory study of the behavior of voluntary hospitals has been done by Kenneth Clarkson.[19] His theory is at least susceptible to empirical validation. Clarkson focused his attention on the way that different organizational structures affect property rights of owners and how this in turn affects economic behavior and the allocation of resources within organizations. Specifically he addresses the attenuation of certain property rights in voluntary hospitals. Owners of proprietary (for profit) hospitals have complete control over such hospitals' assets, including any residual from operations or rights to future benefits which may be produced. Owners or trustees of voluntary hospitals, on the other hand, have no such resalable claim. This being true, managers of these enterprises should expect a smaller reward from the owners for efficient operation (that is, they bear a lower cost for wasteful operations). They should also expect less effective policing of their own performance. Such expectations are presumed to follow from the law of demand. As the pecuniary rewards of efficient operation to owners of voluntary hospitals are less than are these rewards to owners of proprietaries, voluntary hospital owners can be expected to devote less time to monitoring the performance of their hospital managers and to disciplining them with bonuses, profit shares and the like.

Seeking to test the explanatory power of this difference in property rights, Clarkson developed a number of specific implications regarding behavior within hospitals. Among these were predictions that monitoring practices of managers would differ for the two types of organization. In support of this proposition he found that a larger percentage of proprietary hospitals had administrative personnel on duty at night than nonproprietary hospitals and that the amount of time spent on supervisory control was also greater for proprietaries than nonproprietaries.[20] Another implication noted by Clarkson was that managers of nonproprietaries would be less heedful of market information or information of value to the firm than would be managers of proprietaries. In a questionnaire sent to California firms supplying equipment and materials to hospitals, Clarkson found that managers of nonproprietary hospitals tended to be less concerned with the price and productivity of merchandise and more concerned over its "quality," than were managers of proprietaries.[21] Nonproprietaries were also observed to rely more on opinion polls and less on market information such as queues or quit rates for demand and supply data. Automatic salary increases were granted far more frequently by nonproprietary than by proprietary hospitals.[22]

Finally, as managers of nonproprietary hospitals are for the above reasons more likely to deviate from least-cost production techniques, it is predicted that variability of costs and input selection should be greater for these hospitals than for proprietary hospitals. Support for this implication was found in an industry wage survey in which variances of earnings by worker classification were compared. Support was reported in data comparing variance in the men-to-women ratio among the two types of hospital. The variations in various factors and cost ratios for a selected sample of short-term general hospitals were compared, which also supported the variability implication.

Numerous writers have developed reasons why voluntary hospitals may be expected to produce less efficiently than proprietary hospitals. The medical profession may be imposing restrictions which prevent hospitals or hospital-based institutions from offering care which is competitive with physician care. Opportunities to offer lower cost alternatives to the conventional physician visit are prevented by the American Medical Association's sanctions and state laws. In addition, managers of voluntary hospitals may have weaker incentives to manage effectively, that is, to produce the type of care desired by patients at lowest cost. Because owners of voluntary hospitals have attenuated rights to profits of such hospitals, they have less incentive to monitor output and costs. On the contrary, this managerial vacuum left by owner disinterest may be filled by the hospital medical staff. The medical staff may influence hospital management to use hospital donations for the purchase of uneconomic equipment that serves merely to extend unnecessarily each physician's range of services. Rather than give up patients to physicians on the staffs of other hospitals already equipped for such procedures, physicians whose hospitals lack items of equipment devote donated funds to this purpose.

The theory elucidating the efficient use of donated funds has not been written yet, and speculations about the theory are more suited to the talents of a clairvoyant than to those of a theorist. Nevertheless, one may hypothesize that the intentions of hospital donors are better served by expenditure of their contributions to defray costs of extending modest but effective care to those otherwise unable to purchase it, rather than to add a redundant open-heart surgery unit to a community. Privately donated subsidies may, after all, be used to extend output in several dimensions. They may be used to lower the cost of offering more of the same care, to lower the cost of care to certain people, or to lower the cost of services not currently provided. My guess is that, of these three uses, excessive amounts are currently being devoted to lowering the cost in the third of these dimensions.

Hospital Planning

A number of writers have leapt from the observation of alleged waste in connection with the existing, largely voluntary hospital structure in this country to the conclusion that some sort of state imposed "rationalization" of investment decision is called for. They demand planning "with teeth." [23] Such demands are at best premature. They may, even if their underlying premises are true, offer a second best solution. Quite conceivably, they may make matters even worse than they are already.

First, would-be hospital planners are quite vague about the manner in which they expect planners actually to determine an efficient distribution of hospital capacity and equipment over communities. The evaluation of investment projects, even when the objectives of all investors are identical and clear-cut, requires rather sophisticated forecasting and analysis. Such forecasts are frequently mistaken, even under ideal conditions. Where the interest of the various members of the planning commission are likely to be opposed, where the stated objectives of these bodies are vague or empty, and where effectiveness in planning is not likely to be particularly enriching, the prognosis for such planning is not optimistic.

Newhouse and Acton have addressed the question of predicting the effectiveness of planning and regulation of hospitals and conclude that such efforts will be "not very successful." [24] In support of this prediction they note first the considerable number of uncertainties associated with a growing demand for medical services fed in large part by increasing government financing of these services. They also cite the recommendation of the Willink Committee in Great Britain that medical schools reduce admissions in the late 1950s as a case in point. This decision was of necessity reversed and admissions were expanded in the 1960s after it became apparent that the original forecast was based on incorrect assumptions regarding retirement rates and population changes. Newhouse and Acton argue that such errors have a much more severe import when they are incorporated into national planning policy than when they are made by decentralized individual firms making their own projections. An analogy with the "law of large numbers" is invoked to argue that mistakes are less costly, on average, in the latter situation.

Newhouse and Acton also support their contentions with a review of studies of hospital regulation in the past. Of the three studies cited,[25] none indicated that regulation had any effect on the investment behavior of the hospitals considered. The study by Joel May which examined the effectiveness of several planning commissions in reducing "unnecessary" capital expenditures reports no significant positive effect and some perverse effects of regulation.[26] Studies of regulation of other industries were also cited to reinforce this view of the ineffectiveness of regulatory bodies.[27]

We are advised by health planners to adopt a system of economic organization which, viewed sympathetically, is unproven and which many would argue is likely to result in perverse change, if any. The underlying problem here is one which pervades policy-oriented analysis of existing institutions. The results of the operation of these institutions are measured against a yardstick wrought from purely abstract analysis. When these institutions fail to measure up in such comparisons, the analyst announces discovery of a "market failure" and considers the desirability of planning to be self-evident. Little space is devoted to a similar search for planning failures which, as we have seen, are a factor to be reckoned with. It is not surprising that, when the operation of real world institutions is compared with perfection, shortcomings are identified.

On the other hand, evidence is beginning to accumulate that there is an alternative organizational form for hospitals which does operate more efficiently than the conventional voluntary hospital organization. Evidence reviewed above supports this view. Here economies in operation are suggested both by economic theory and by comparisons of the actual performance of both organizational forms. Arguments against proprietary organization have been considered above and have generally been found to be unconvincing.

In comparing organizational forms for hospitals, support exists for the view that improved performance might be obtained by shifting from voluntary organization to proprietary organization, that is, by selling off hospitals to firms interested in operating them for profit. The question remains whether similar (or greater) gains might be obtained by superimposing central planning and direction over the existing unplanned, largely voluntary, hospital structure. Lacking an empirically useful model of a community-planned system, our ability to analyze such propositions is limited. Experience with planning and regulation has not been encouraging.

In the next chapter the operation of government hospitals will be explored. Frequently individual hospitals are part of a larger government hospital system. Analysis of these systems will, to a certain extent at least, inform us about the expected performance of hospitals that are part of a centrally planned system.

CHAPTER III

GOVERNMENT HOSPITALS

Still to be considered is the hospital organization structure of government-operated hospitals, particularly the VA hospitals focused on in this study. Even more often than is the case with nonprofit, voluntary hospitals, the administrator of a government hospital fills an ambiguous role. Like all such administrators, public and private, he is charged with selecting (within varying degrees of discretion) the combination of quality and quantity to be produced with his allotted budget. His role differs from that of his counterpart in proprietary hospitals in two important respects. First, he must rely on a different source of information concerning desired characteristics of the output to be produced by his bureau. The second difference lies in the sources of information on which those with supervisory responsibility over these managers must rely to gauge their performance as managers.

The typical study seeking to assess the performance of government agencies or enterprises attempts to compare their costs with costs experienced by private firms producing similar products. As noted in Chapter I, such comparisons almost invariably are confounded by quality differences in government and private output. One may deal with this problem in two ways. The most straightforward way is to estimate a second cost variable, the cost of quality independent of output, in such a way that costs of outputs of different quality may be made comparable. This can be done only where a suitable index of quality exists and where quality can be measured. For output as varied and complex as that of modern hospitals, no such index exists.

A second way of dealing with this problem, of necessity the approach taken here, is to allow quality differences themselves to drive the analysis. If quality differences between government and private output are systematically observed, then an economic explanation for such differences may exist which itself may provide information useful to this analysis.

The term *quality* itself must be subjected to scrutiny before it becomes the focal point of this analysis. Quality cannot be discussed meaningfully without recognizing the multidimensional character of nearly all goods and services. For example, a hospital day (frequently used as the unit of output) must realistically be considered a vector of many product characteristics. These would include a quantity of nurse and physician visits, the use of some amount of hospital space and equipment, quantities of laboratory and radiological work, as well as food preparation and other hotel-like services. Each of these characteristics in turn may be broken down into even more basic product characteristics such as quantities of pulse and temperature recordings, number of blood cultures or chest x-rays, and quantities of lunches and dinners. Quality is typically interpreted as the ratio of the quantities of ancillary attributes to some basic characteristic giving the good or service its identity. For example, high quality in a hospital day of care would suggest, in the output vector of a hospital, a high ratio of nurses' visits, lab work, et cetera, to bed days.

The following analysis will attempt to generate propositions which suggest that the mode of organization (that is, proprietary or governmental) will itself influence the choice of the level of various output characteristics in predictable ways. It will be shown that the influence of the governmental mode results in an inefficient, and typically lower, level of quality than that provided by proprietary hospitals. Thus it stands in contrast to earlier work which suggests that managers of nonprofit institutions will choose to provide inefficiently high levels of quality.[1]

Democratic Guidance

Managers of proprietary hospitals interested in earning profits from their enterprises look to the market for information on the proper mix of output characteristics. By experimentation and observation of the profit performance of rivals, these managers may discover profitable modifications in the current output vector. Ability to glean such information from the market is a mark of effective private management. Because profits are assumed to be the only concern of the owners, the path to success for such managers is quite straight-forward.

The successful administrator of government enterprises does not attempt to maximize profits. His success depends on pleasing those responsible for monitoring the administrator. But in government, it must be presumed, no weight is assigned to the accounting profits of a bureau by officials monitoring the performance of such managers. Indeed, the output of many government enterprises is made available at zero price. Market information concerning product quality (that is, willingness of customers to pay more for modified products) is therefore of little use to these administrators. These managers look instead to government officials for guidance concerning the desired level and quality of their outputs.

In democratic nations, government officials presumably look in turn to the electorate for this information. Congress, for example, seeks to implement the type of medical benefit program for veterans that is desired by the American public. Congress may be viewed as being merely the interpreter of the popular will in this regard, urging administrators to provide a combination of output characteristics which they perceive to be desired, and rewarding them on the basis of their efficiency in doing so. Even under the most ideal circumstances imaginable, one would expect Congress, or any such elected body, to be a very imperfect conduit of such information. Elected officials must supply similar guidance to all government enterprises. The time they might be expected to devote to obtaining a clear determination of the wishes of the public regarding such details for each government activity is of necessity quite limited. The short time horizon faced by most elected officials also contributes to the lack of expertise on the part of those who must supply this guidance.

Thus, even if the public were of one mind concerning the output desired from such enterprises, one would predict considerable error in the characteristics of output supplied. But clearly the public itself is not likely to be in perfect agreement on this issue. On the contrary, such agreement is particularly unlikely in the case of the VA hospital program that provides services to only a subset of the total voting public whose eligibility is based on widely varying criteria.

To the disabled combatants (that is, the service-connected patients), the desirable mix of services would be a low level of output concentrated on themselves. These voters would be willing to sacrifice little quality in the care administered to service-connected cases to gain more quantity for distribution to other potentially eligible veterans. On the other hand the second group of veterans is eligible to receive hospitalization only on a space-available basis, and they hope to receive hospitalization of high quality, too. They recognize, however, that if too much capacity is sacrificed in the interests of quality, their chances of finding available space will be greatly diminished. We would therefore predict that this group would support a quite different combination of quality and quantity than would the former group. Thirdly, there is the non-veteran group of voters whose concern for veteran benefit programs is completely compassionate. It seems plausible that these voters might be more inclined to side with the service-connected group above.

To whom do the politicians—and thus, after a fashion, the administrators—respond in this matter? This is difficult to say, particularly when the competing groups are large and politically potent, as is the case here. In any event, however the political issue is resolved among these competing factions, it is highly unlikely that any group will admit satisfaction with the combination of capacity and quality chosen. Representatives of veterans' groups, which are largely composed of veterans with no service-connected disability, would probably favor broadening the eligible population (for example, by extending medical care privileges to families of veterans, and increasing hospital capacity). Those with service-connected conditions requiring treatment would at the same time seek to prevent the extension of eligibility and to upgrade the quality of the services provided.

One might speculate that the crowded conditions noted in many VA hospitals may result, at least in part, from the interaction of these two groups. The disabled combatant group tries to limit the amount of non-service-connected care dispensed by VA hospitals by limiting VA expenditures for expansion of physical facilities. Members of the non-service-connected veteran group can be expected, on the other hand, to prefer heavily subsidized care, even provided under crowded conditions, to care financed by themselves. They thus apply pressure through their organizations to gain admission to hospitals already filled in terms of higher quality standards. Hence, any particular hospital in the VA system may look different to members of these two groups. To the group wishing to provide high-quality care for wounded veterans, such a hospital may appear filled to capacity. To the non-service-connected veteran seeking admission to such a hospital it may seem to exhibit space available. Success by this latter group in gaining admission under these circumstances would lead, predictably, to expressions of dissatisfaction among the former regarding the overcrowding of facilities.

Monitoring Costs

The second difference in the role of the private and public manager concerns the kinds of information available to those who evaluate the manager's performance. This difference also suggests that efficiency suffers under government organization: the owners of private companies acquire a great deal of information concerning the productivity of their management by observing the profits of their own and similar companies. If their own profit performance suffers in such comparisons, the owners may suspect that the manager is comparatively ineffective and replace him or lower his salary.

The productivity of managers of government enterprises cannot be measured in this way, because government enterprises do not attempt to maximize profits. Thus, even were profit information available on such operations, it would not be particularly useful for evaluating management. Those responsible for monitoring the performance of these managers must attempt, usually without benefit of comparison with competing enterprises, to assess directly management's ability to combine factors efficiently and produce the desired output. Even when comparisons are possible between private and government enterprises that supply the same product, relevant data is very costly to obtain. As we pointed out in Chapter I, the efficiency of government enterprises is almost impossible to gauge directly, even when the same product is produced privately or by some other agency of government. Although the products produced in either case may in some sense be the same, we have already noted the extreme difficulty of adjusting for quality differences in ways which make such comparisons meaningful. Owners of private firms need not make the heavy investment in information required for sophisticated evaluations of productivity. They need only compare their company's current profits with profits from previous years and profits of competing companies to measure with considerable precision the effectiveness of their own management.

In the absence of profit information, those who monitor managers must develop alternative indicators of the efficiency of government enterprises. The "paper mill" bureaucracy frequently deplored by observers of government organization is a manifestation of this need for information to be supplied to those at the top. Without such red tape, government officials and private citizens would have no way of gauging the efficiency with which appropriations are spent.

The fact that statistical reports take the place of profit information in the government bureaucracy does not imply that this substitution is functionally perfect, however. On the contrary, it is well-known among observers of the performance of the centrally directed economies of eastern Europe that the cost of obtaining sufficient information to indicate accurately the success (that is, productivity) of enterprise management is frequently prohibitive.[2] Attempts to assess the efficiency of a government enterprise typically take the form of average-cost calculations. It goes without saying that this statistic is a faulty indicator of the appropriate decision variable, marginal cost, but this is a minor problem. When success is indicated by low average cost alone, it is in the interest of managers to lower cost in every possible way including lowering the quality of the product itself. The fact that the output of such enterprises is usually dispensed at zero price means that information which typically serves as a check on this behavior in private firms and in eastern Europe, that is, inventory buildup of inferior merchandise, is not available to government officials here. Manager-directed quality deterioration in the product may only be detected by costly inspection.

Predictably, quality deterioration would take a number of forms in the VA hospital system. Perhaps the most obvious avenue for false economies lies in reduction of the professional staff. Theory suggests that among hospitals with similar patient populations the ratio of medical doctors and nurses to patients is likely to be lower in government hospitals than in proprietary hospitals, where consumer sovereignty would be expected to deter such quality depreciation. Although this proposition is difficult to test because of the dissimilarity of VA and proprietary hospital populations, some support may be found in Table 5. For the years surveyed staff to patient ratios for proprietary hospitals are consistently more than 70 percent higher than staff to patient ratios of VA hospitals.

The same argument clearly holds for building space and equipment. Average costs in terms of patient days of care may be reduced by cutting back on building and equipment services provided to patients, that is, by crowding wards and providing less equipment. Because such reductions in the quality of the patient days may only be detected by repeated on-site inspections and thus only by specialists trained to recognize such deficiencies, we may predict that such opportunities are exploited by managers of government enterprises. Although there seems to be no statistical evidence comparing floor space or equipment to patient ratios among government and proprietary hospitals, much of the recent testimony before Congress reviewed in Chapter I appears consistent with such a prediction.[3]

42

Table 5
STAFF-PATIENT RATIOS FOR VA AND PROPRIETARY HOSPITALS: 1969–1973

Year	VA General Hospitals	Proprietary Short-term General Hospitals
1969	1.42	2.44
1970	1.46	2.56
1971	n.a.	2.62
1972	n.a.	2.67
1973	1.59	2.72

Source: U.S. House of Representatives, Committee on Veterans' Affairs, *Operations of Veterans Administration Hospitals and Medical Program,* various years, and *Hospitals, Guide Issue* 1969–1973.

It may be legitimately objected at this point that low personnel to patient ratios and reports of "overcrowding" of facilities are a matter of public record, and that elected officials need go no farther than their daily newspaper to discover that quality is being depreciated in this manner. Indeed, formal channels of direct communication between individual VA hospitals and the House Committee on Veterans' Affairs have existed since 1952. One might ask then why reports themselves do not prevent deterioration of quality. The answer is that ultimately it is personnel and equipment *services* that are important characteristics of output. Although elected officials may easily observe the amount of labor and equipment inputs used, they may not economically monitor the output of the services of these factors. When output (services) is unmonitored, managers have no economic incentive to use input (resources) productively. Elected officials, on the other hand, being aware of the lack of such incentives, attach little importance to observations that input levels are comparatively low. They are not anxious to permit bureaucrats to waste large quantities of these resources. The use of inputs as a proxy for outputs in the gauging of productivity has long been recognized as an incentive to waste, and we might expect Congress to try to limit the resources subject only to this type of monitoring practice.

A more subtle avenue for cost reduction via quality depreciation is the hiring of less productive and therefore less costly inputs, particularly professional personnel. The fact that on average certain medical and nursing staffs are less distinguished and less qualified than others need not of course imply that the quality of care they provide is relatively low. There is presumably some rate of technical substitution of high- for low-productivity personnel that will allow quality and output to be held constant despite such changes. The average productivity of inputs alone is not an unambiguous indicator of the quality of output, but differences in input productivity do, however, inform us regarding the quality of output, all else being equal. Reported average costs (and output quality) are lowered by the substitution on a one-for-one basis of less qualified and thus less productive medical and nursing staff for more qualified and thus more costly counterparts.

Consider the following situation: Those who must monitor the administrator of a hospital are aware that he will attempt to lower average cost by hiring fewer personnel. They may seek to check this quality depreciation by requiring that he report, in addition to average cost, the ratio of physicians, nurses, and other personnel to patients. They may further enjoin such administrators from allowing these ratios to drop below minimum levels which they establish. Administrators thus constrained retain the option of reducing average cost by substituting lower productivity inputs for higher productivity inputs, however. Since VA regulations do stipulate minimum personnel to patient ratios, we can predict that managers of VA hospitals will tend to hire personnel with lower productivity on average.[4]

Such a tendency is difficult to document with confidence, because objective measures of the skill and knowledge of hospital personnel are costly to implement, and the information is not otherwise readily available. Three proxies for such productivity differences indicate that this tendency prevails in VA hospitals, however. First, average earnings of VA physicians are significantly below the average earnings of all American physicians. The mean salary of full-time VA physicians was roughly $31,000 in 1973. The top scale for these physicians was $36,000 per year.[5] Average net earnings for the profession as a whole were greater than $31,000 per year in 1968 and were growing at a rate of between 8.4 percent and 11.4 percent per year.[6] Mean net earnings of all physicians were reported to be $39,700 in 1969.[7] Average salaries for full-time VA physicians were less than $25,000 in that year.

Secondly, it is widely argued that foreign medical schools are usually inferior to American medical schools. Assuming this to be true, we can predict that VA hospitals will employ a larger proportion of graduates of foreign medical schools than the proportion that practices in private hospitals. The proportion of VA physicians holding degrees from foreign medical schools was 25 percent in 1970.

Foreign-trained physicians represented 17 percent of all those licensed in the United States in the same year.[8]

Finally, there remains the VA hospitals' performance as recruiters in terms of their own perceptions of productivity (or, as they prefer to refer to it, qualifications). In published responses to a Congressional questionnaire that was sent to all VA hospitals requesting information on their "needs," there were repeated references to "the inability to recruit and retain well-qualified physicians." The VA hospital at Salisbury, North Carolina, remarked, "Another great need of this hospital is a salary scale for physicians which would permit us to successfully recruit top-flight doctors." [9]

A systematic study of the VA's performance in the national intern matching program would prove highly revealing on this score. In this program hospitals and applicant interns rank each other and are then matched by computer. Applicants for intern positions name their most favored five or six hospitals in order of preference and hospitals rank applicants from 1 through 100. A study of these results would provide objective evidence regarding one aspect of VA hospital recruiting. This kind of study has not been done to my knowledge and is beyond the scope of this work. It may be revealing in this connection that Wadsworth, a VA hospital in a large metropolitan area (Los Angeles) with prestigious medical school connections (UCLA), recently hired its ninety-eighth choice.[10]

One final example will be cited of behavior demonstrating that VA managers seek to lower costs by reducing personal service to patients. VA regulations provide that outpatients be given advance appointments for visits to clinics whenever possible. It is customary for physicians in private practice offering outpatient care to schedule appointments for their patients. At many VA outpatient facilities, however, no appointments are made at all. Typically patients are advised to report at 8:00 a.m. if they wish to be seen before noon and to report at 1:00 p.m. if they wish to be seen in the afternoon. The General Accounting Office (GAO) has reported that the average waiting time among such patients is approximately one and one-half hours. Some veterans must wait the full four hours to be seen.[11]

The reason for failure to schedule appointments for outpatients has been succinctly stated by an official at one of the VA hospitals that has ignored the directive to provide appointments. The official said that "having all outpatients report at the opening of the clinic maximized the physicians' [productivity], because physicians' time is wasted when specific time appointments are not kept." [12] Of little concern to such administrators, apparently, is the amount of time wasted by patients waiting for care in such clinics.

Thus far, we have considered the implications of government organization of activity concerned primarily with the analysis of inputs. The theory developed here suggests that managers of government enterprises will attempt to divert resources from the production of invisible characteristics of output (those which are costly to monitor) toward the production of those which are visible (easily monitored). Patient-days of care are closely monitored, while professional and capital services supplied to patients cannot be, nor can the productivity of those services, nor the use of patient time. The observation that VA managers have economized on the production of this invisible output is therefore consistent with this model.

A second opportunity to substitute visible for invisible output occurs in conjunction with the ability of VA hospitals to choose their patients. Those veterans whose disabilities the VA is obliged to treat comprise only about 7 percent of the total veteran population. The remaining 93 percent are admitted and treated on a space-available basis. Cost per patient-day is clearly lower for hospitals filled with patients requiring little care than for hospitals filled with acute cases. VA hospital managers may be expected to adopt policies that tend to fill their hospitals with patients whose care is least costly in an effort to lower costs per patient-day. Well patients represent the ideal from this point of view, because they presumably need no care at all beyond so-called hotel services. Thus it is not surprising that many beds in VA hospitals are indeed filled by patients who do not require hospitalization at all, but who are admitted for tests or examinations that might be satisfactorily performed using out-patient facilities.

Excessive stays by those with conditions legitimately requiring hospitalization are also predicted. Table 6 shows that, on average, patients in VA hospitals do remain hospitalized longer when undergoing a given surgical procedure than do patients in private hospitals. The finding of longer stays for VA patients was systematic across ages. The range of ages reported on here is that most typical of VA patient populations.

A recent GAO survey of medical records from six VA hospitals reported that, of the 420 files reviewed, seventy-nine cases of excessive utilization were discovered.[13] In these cases hospitalization might have been shortened by moving the patients to nursing homes or treating them as outpatients. When this kind of excess utilization was projected to all admissions at the six hospitals surveyed, it was estimated that 86,000 days of hospitalization might have been eliminated during the test year.[14]

Table 6

AVERAGE LENGTHS OF STAY IN VA AND VOLUNTARY
HOSPITALS, BY SURGICAL PROCEDURE, FOR PATIENTS
AGE 50–64 EXCEPT WHERE NOTED

(reported by days)

Procedure	VA	Voluntary
Pilonidal cyst (age 35-49)	15.7	5.8
Diabetes mellitus	19.0	9.0
Acute coronary occlusion	31.5	21.7
Hemorrhoidectomy	15.8	7.1
Tonsils and adenoids (age 35-49)	6.4	2.4
Duodenum ulcer	15.2	6.7
Appendicitis	12.1	6.9
Inguinal hernia	17.1	7.2
Gastroenteritis and colitis	11.1	7.7
Gallstones	26.5	11.9
Pyelitis, cystitis, nephritis	11.6	6.0
Kidney stones	18.6	8.2
Prostate	22.1	9.7

Source: Interagency Length of Stay Study Group (unpublished). Some results published in U.S. House of Representatives, Committee on Veterans Affairs, *Veterans Administration Hospital Funding and Personnel Needs,* 91st Congress, 2d Session, 1970, p. 3347.

An example of this bureaucratic over-hospitalization revealed by the GAO survey was cited in the report. A veteran originally admitted for swollen ankles diagnosed as heart trouble was discovered the day after admission to be suffering from a circulatory problem in the lower extremities. The treating physician agreed with the GAO survey team that the patient might have been treated from that point on as an outpatient, avoiding in the process thirteen unnecessary days of hospital care. The GAO reports that the patient was not released "because there was no administrative pressure to release patients to outpatient care. The physician decided to treat the patient in the hospital rather than having him return for outpatient visits even though the veteran lived only five miles away." [15] This "lack of administrative pressure" is understandable when one considers that the release of such a patient may free a hospital bed for an acutely ill patient who requires considerable amounts of expensive care.

Another category of well patients who fill bed space is the group of patients awaiting surgery. The GAO reports that in none of the six hospitals visited had procedures been established to coordinate patient admission with the availability of surgical facilities. In each case surgery was scheduled after a patient was admitted, resulting in unnecessary hospitalizations of up to a week by patients awaiting surgery. It was noted that in a private hospital contacted by the GAO, surgery dates are established prior to admission and patients are invariably operated on the day after admission. The GAO estimates that such delays account annually for 15,000 unnecessary days of hospitalization in the six hospitals surveyed alone.

The following case was cited by the GAO as an example of such avoidable hospitalization:

> A veteran was seen by the admitting physician on October 8, 1970, who determined that the patient had a hernia and needed surgery. He was admitted to the hospital on October 28, 1970. A specific surgery date was not scheduled before he was admitted. The veteran had to wait 9 days after admission for the hernia operation since surgical time was not available at an earlier date. The treating physician advised us that at least 7 days of hospitalization could have been avoided if the admission date had been coordinated with the availability of surgical times. This would have reduced the total hospital stay from 14 to 7 days.[16]

The effect of this incentive structure extends beyond extreme cases such as those identified by the GAO. Indeed the possibility of reducing reported average cost by altering the composition of the patient population may explain, at least in part, the remarkably high proportion of chronic, as opposed to acute, cases treated in VA hospitals. Other factors such as the remoteness of VA hospitals and the age distribution of veterans in general doubtless contribute to this tendency. Nevertheless, less than 10 percent of all veterans treated for appendicitis, fractures, dislocations, and upper respiratory conditions are treated in VA hospitals, while 33 percent of arthritis cases and 35 percent of mental disorders are treated in VA hospitals.[17] The fact that the cost per patient-day of treating cases in the first category is higher than that of treating cases in the latter category cannot be discounted as a contributing factor toward this difference in utilization.

Indeed, the question of utilization has been raised in two separate examinations by the Joint Committee on Accreditation of Hospitals.[18] In both 1970 and 1971 the commission identified "utilization review" as an area in need of improvement. The commission concluded that the VA's utilization review procedures should be expanded to better determine whether "the resources of the hospital—both plant and personnel—were appropriately utilized." [19] The GAO's own review of the minutes of utilization review committee meetings at two VA hospitals elicited the following remarks:

> Most comments were directed toward the accuracy of medical records rather than the efficiency of patient care. For example, most of the committees' comments concerned adequacy of medical history, length of medical summary and legibility of handwriting. In a few cases where questions were raised concerning utilization, we found that action was usually taken to correct the problem identified only in the specific case. Efforts were not made to identify trends and patterns of utilization problems to make recommendations for correcting the causes of identified problems. [20]

In total the GAO estimated that, as a result of the inefficient practices which they identified, 146,000, or 15 percent, of the one million days furnished at the six hospitals surveyed could have been avoided. Extrapolating this percentage over the entire VA hospital system suggests that the cost of these practices may indeed be enormous. The Veterans Administration provides currently more than 30 million patient-days of care. Fifteen percent of this total would imply a savings of more than 4.5 million patient-days of unnecessary hospitalization. Converting this to hospital beds by recalling that the VA hospital occupancy rate is approximately 84 percent, this suggests that 14,677 hospital beds in the VA system are needlessly occupied.

Recall, however, that this excess utilization identified by the GAO is perhaps only the most visible effect of this incentive structure. The total cost of patient substitution to reduce average cost is difficult to reckon. The larger cost may *not* be the excess hospitalization identified by the GAO, but rather the fact that, on the whole, the Veterans Administration is treating a different patient population than that intended for it by the public. Certainly if the public wishes to make available for veterans a package of medical services similar to that consumed by the average citizen, then these wishes are apparently being thwarted. The VA care currently being delivered is much more heavily weighted toward chronic care than that provided in non-government hospitals. However, we shall leave to the next two chapters consideration of the larger objectives of the VA hospital system and alternative means of satisfying them.

Property Rights and Hospital Management

As a nonproprietary hospital, a government hospital is predicted also to experience the difficulties identified by Clarkson in connection with voluntary hospitals (discussed in Chapter II) which arise from attenuation of the property rights of owners. Propositions suggested by this approach were that (1) supervisory and administrative personnel of nonproprietaries would spend less time monitoring the behavior of other personnel, (2) they would devote less time to the gathering of market information of value to the hospital, (3) automatic pay raises for personnel of nonproprietaries would be observed more frequently (that is, attempts to relate wages to productivity would be less vigorous), and (4) greater variability in the cost of production of these hospitals should be observed. Clarkson produced convincing empirical support for each of these propositions regarding government as well as nonprofit voluntary hospitals.[21]

As is the case with voluntary hospitals, owners of government hospitals have no rights to profits and future benefits provided by these hospitals. Indeed, one has difficulty identifying someone who fills the role of owner in the case of government enterprises. Ultimately, perhaps, members of the general public may be considered the owners, but their control over the fortunes of such enterprises is tenuous at best. As profits of such enterprises are never distributed, the interest of such owners in efficient operation is attenuated. Cost savings generated by efficient management may yield a budget surplus—to be spent to provide different benefits or tax savings to others. The share of such cost savings assured to vigilant investors in proprietary firms in the form of a capital gain is never paid by government enterprises. Lacking these rewards, citizen owners devote fewer resources to the monitoring of the management of government enterprises. These managers in turn have less incentive to manage effectively.

The predicted result of such an attenuation of rights is less efficient operation. Measurement of this difference in efficiency is very costly for the reasons we have already discussed at length. In addition to the incentives operating to influence administrators to devote fewer resources to management, other factors influence them to change the quality of the product offered. Mere comparisons of average cost are thus likely to produce an unrealistically sanguine view of the efficiency of such operations. Indeed, as reported earlier, average cost comparisons of VA with private hospitals do not reflect unfavorably on the *apparent* efficiency of VA hospital operations. However, since these figures—even if accounting differences are ignored—measure the costs of radically different products, little confidence may be placed in such comparisons.

As was noted by Clarkson, associated effects of inefficiency may be revealed in other characteristics of nonproprietary hospital behavior. One such effect predicted by Clarkson was that the variance in costs among nonproprietary hospitals should be higher. Clarkson argues that, if nonproprietary hospital management has less incentive to choose the lowest-cost combination of inputs, then costs are likely to vary more among these hospitals and over time than they do for proprietary hospitals which are continuously under greater pressure to economize. Clarkson, as we have noted, found evidence that the variance in nonproprietary hospital costs was significantly larger than the variance in proprietary hospital costs.

Similar evidence generated from VA reports also supports this hypothesis of greater variability of cost among government (nonproprietary) hospitals. In Table 3 the standard deviation of the per diem costs of VA-operated nursing homes was shown to be almost four times the standard deviation of per diem costs incurred by the Veterans Administration when patients are placed in community nursing homes. In the case of nursing home care, considered in this example, even average-cost comparisons reflect unfavorably on the governmental organizational form.

Considerable waste due to poor management was also reported in the GAO report discussed extensively above. Perhaps the most flagrant example of this concerned the disposition of reports of medical tests performed on patients being admitted to VA hospitals. The GAO reports that many such tests were ordered and performed twice simply because those ordered by admitting physicians were delayed in being placed in the patient's file. To test the timeliness of the filing of such reports, the GAO examined a sample of such test results. It found that the average delay in placing such results in the appropriate patient's file was thirty days after the tests were completed. In one case observed in the sample, the results remained unfiled for 181 days.[22]

Summary

Thus, government enterprises suffer in general from two critical information problems. First, the lack of sales and profit information for managers implies that reliance must be placed on busy elected officials for details concerning characteristics and quality of the services demanded. Even where there is consensus among the public regarding the desirable mix of levels and quality of all the services provided, we can be certain that this information would be imperfectly transmitted through the machinery of government to administrators of the program. These administrators, in receipt of ambiguous guidance, cannot be expected to select the ideal level of each variable under their control.

In this particular case, however, ambiguity surrounds even the concept of "ideal level." Different political coalitions will probably desire different combinations of output, quality, and so forth. As elections change government personnel, official views regarding these decisions may also change and with them the messages transmitted (imperfectly in the first place) to bureau administrators. Under these circumstances one cannot but conclude that the mix of quantities and qualities ultimately chosen is likely to be different from the appropriate level, however defined.

A second information problem also impedes efficient provision of hospital services through government-operated hospitals. This is the problem of gauging the productivity of inputs in government enterprises, or, viewed from a slightly different vantage point, measuring the effectiveness of the management of such operations. Because much of the output is offered at zero price or at prices which are not intended to cover cost, profit calculations do not reveal the efficiency of the enterprise or the productivity of its management. Those responsible for monitoring the performance of these managers must rely on information developed independently through reports from management and the customers. Neither of these sources can be expected to provide unbiased information. Furthermore, such information is costly to obtain, particularly in cases such as hospital organization in which output is not a single product with a few readily measurable characteristics but rather a broad spectrum of complex services, none of which is truly comparable with those provided by other types of hospitals, and all of which are offered under excess demand (shortage) conditions.

The least costly information to obtain is total variable cost, which may be compared with a number of surrogates for output such as patient-days or cases treated to yield average costs of a sort. The most costly information to gather concerns the quality of output. Patients do not reveal their valuations of the product purchased in the prices they pay, and samplings of patient opinion are likely to be biased downward.

Under these circumstances, it seems reasonable to expect that managers will attempt to allocate resources under their control in such a way that average cost, which is most closely monitored, is minimized at the expense of quality, which can be monitored only imperfectly. A number of ways in which this might be done have been suggested in this chapter. Indications that such opportunities are exploited by some echelon of VA or government administration were reported and examined.

Opportunities for reducing cost by reducing output quality include (1) decreasing the number and quality of the inputs per unit of measured output (that is, reducing staff quantity and quality, crowding, and failing to maintain physical facilities), (2) minimizing slack periods for professional staff by eliminating appointments and requiring patients to queue for services, (3) selecting patients on the basis of predicted cost of treatment including unwarranted hospitalization of patients requiring only tests or outpatient treatment, excessive stays by those with legitimate hospital needs, and preference for patients with chronic disorders which are likely to involve lower costs per day than do acute cases.

The foregoing is not intended to suggest that administrators and managers of the Veterans Administration medical care program are perverse, incompetent or lack dedication to serving the needs of veterans. Economics is a science in which differences in personality, ability and tastes play little part, and this economic assessment reflects the organizational scheme in which incentives, indeed *survival characteristics*, facing management leave little discretion. An improvement in the quality of the care provided will increase cost. The increase in quality may not be apparent to higher administrators. The increase in cost almost certainly will be.

The perplexed bureaucrat does not lack comforting rationalizations for his behavior. Needlessly admitting a patient or prolonging hospitalization typically is a matter of considerable convenience and savings to the patient himself. Often the alternative is outpatient care which the patient himself must finance. The hardship faced by the individual concerned is immediate and apparent. The cost in terms of space denied to a patient with more acute hospital needs is less visible and often confused with the desire for larger capacity. Similarly crowding and understaffing are easy to rationalize in terms of attempting to fill some of these unmet needs.

Unmet needs are unlikely ever to be satisfied by any plausible capacity provided by the Veterans Administration, however. It is not the intention of Congress to provide for all the hospital needs of all veterans. VA hospitals exist to treat service-connected wounds, illnesses, and injuries. Other care is extended on a space-available basis to the veteran population.

Hospital administrators cannot, therefore, avoid setting priorities for allocating the beds available—that is, denying space to some of those who need it. Crowding reduces the quality of care to those who receive it, including the primary population the hospitals are presumably intended to serve. Whether the inconvenience of crowding those with service-connected conditions is offset by the gains experienced by the additional patients treated is a judgment left to the hospital administrator. It is argued here that such a judgment will be colored by the fact that crowding will reduce average cost and give the appearance of increased efficiency.

Actual performance of government hospitals and therefore VA hospitals is predicted to be less efficient than proprietary hospitals. Clarkson has produced evidence that government hospitals *do* operate in general less efficiently. Additional evidence developed above concerning VA operations themselves is consistent with this hypothesis.

CHAPTER IV

ALTERNATIVES TO GOVERNMENT HOSPITAL CARE

To this point discussion of the Veterans Administration medical system has been confined to consideration of how the system is predicted to perform and has performed in its acknowledged role as a provider of medical care to veterans. Discussion of alternatives to this system has been limited thus far to the manner in which the organizational nature of a hospital may be expected to affect its operations. We have, in other words, considered how VA hospitals perform as hospitals. We have yet to consider the larger objectives which are satisfied, in part at least, through the activities of VA hospitals. Here we shall consider the question of whether those larger objectives are indeed effectively served by direct government provision of hospital services.

The VA medical system was established to provide medical care to veterans with a need for hospitalization arising out of wounds, injuries, or illness sustained in connection with military duty. In the process of fulfilling this role, the VA hospital system has, with the passage of time, accrued additional responsibilities. These are the care of veterans with non-service-connected conditions and a recent commitment to participate in and share the cost of financing the training of medical personnel in this country.

Composition of Patient Population in VA Hospitals

The care of veterans with non-service-connected conditions was undertaken as the flow of wounded and disabled World War I veterans began to slacken in the late 1920s and early 1930s. As the number of empty beds increased in VA hospitals, the pressure to fill this space with veterans requiring hospitalization for non-service-connected causes increased. Care was made available to these men on a reimbursable but heavily subsidized basis except for those veterans willing to declare themselves medically indigent. Since that time, care of non-service-connected patients has been transformed from an ancillary function to an increasingly dominant role of the VA medical system.

Care of service-connected conditions, on the other hand, has diminished in importance to the point where it represents a decidedly minor part of VA operations. In spite of the wide press coverage and expressions of official concern regarding the care of returning Vietnam veterans, only 21 percent of living American veterans served on active duty during the Vietnam era. Table 7 presents the distribution of veterans by period of service, listing also the average age of veterans in each category.

Nor do wounded Vietnam veterans represent a large portion of those currently hospitalized. Of the 81,150 patients hospitalized in VA hospitals on a sample day in 1971, only 7,671 (9.5 percent) served during the Vietnam era. The number of these Vietnam era patients who were actually hospitalized for service-connected reasons is not reported but is, of course, at least somewhat less than this. Table 8 lists the numbers of patients remaining in VA hospitals on this sample day in 1971 by period of service.

Table 7
PERIOD OF SERVICE AND ESTIMATED AGE OF VETERANS AS OF 30 JUNE 1972

Period of Service	Number of Veterans (thousands)	Percentage	Average Age
War veterans	25,691	89.2	46.0
Vietnam era	(5,976)	(20.8)	(27.6)
Korean conflict	(5,908)	(20.5)	(43.0)
World War II	(14,122)	(49.0)	(52.6)
World War I	(1,291)	(4.5)	(77.5)
Service between Korean and Vietnam conflicts only	3,113	10.8	33.7
Total veterans	28,804[a]	100.0	44.7

[a] Numbers in this column do not sum to total because of double counting of individuals who participated in more than one conflict.

Source: U.S. Veterans Administration, *Annual Report 1972, Administrator of Veterans Affairs,* p. 99, table 3.

Table 8

PATIENTS REMAINING IN VA HOSPITALS ON
20 OCTOBER 1971, BY PERIOD OF SERVICE

Period of Service	Number	Percentage
Vietnam era	7,671	9.5
Korean conflict	9,131	11.2
World War II	43,978	54.2
World War I	14,088	17.4
All others	6,279	7.7
Total	81,150	100.0

Source: U.S. Veterans Administration, *Annual Report 1972, Administrator of Veterans Affairs*, p. 113, table 16.

Neither returning Vietnam veterans nor the dramatic spinal cord injury patients featured in much of the sensational press coverage discussed in Chapter I are truly representative of the VA patient population. The total number of spinal cord injury patients of all ages in VA hospitals on this sample day was only 2,646 or 3.3 percent of all patients.[1] More than half of these patients received their injuries as civilians or on duty for non-service-connected reasons.

As is clear from Table 8, the majority of all patients present in VA hospitals are veterans of World War II. Furthermore, the representation of this group will probably increase dramatically over the next few years. Public Law 91-500 provides that veterans of World War I and World War II who are sixty-five years of age or older are eligible for VA medical care regardless of service connection. Within the next twenty years virtually all of the 14 million veterans of World War II will become eligible under this law.

Pre-Vietnam patients are not, for the most part, being treated for injuries or illnesses connected with service performed in an earlier period. About 33.7 percent of the patients in VA hospitals on 20 October 1971 were hospitalized as a result of some service-connected health problem. Service connection associated with injury or illness often is an ambiguous matter, however, and admitting physicians must rank an injury or illness on a scale of 1 to 100 percent service-connected. Also included in the service-connected group are cases in which the disabilities specifically treated involve no service connection, but in which the veteran treated has other compensable service-connected disabilities. If patients in this category are eliminated, as well as those designated as exhibiting less than 10 percent service connection, the proportion of the total patient

Table 9

PATIENTS REMAINING IN VA HOSPITALS BY
COMPENSATION STATUS, 20 OCTOBER 1971

Compensation Status	Patients	Percentage
Service-connected conditions	27,348	33.7
More than 10 percent service-connected	(16,779)	(20.7)
Less than 10 percent service-connected	(880)	(1.1)
Non-service-connected with *other* service-connected disability	(9,689)	(11.9)
Non-service-connected conditions	53,313	65.6
Pension	(25,189)	(31.0)
Other	(28,126)	(34.6)
Nonveterans	472	0.6
Total	81,150	100.0

Source: U.S. Veterans Administration, *Annual Report 1972, Administrator of Veterans Affairs,* p. 111, table 15.

population with service-connected disabilities falls to 20.7 percent.[2] Table 9 shows the number of patients in VA hospitals grouped by compensation status in 1971.

Two things are clear about the VA hospital system patient population. Other objectives notwithstanding, VA hospitals are filled primarily by veterans of earlier wars who are being treated for conditions that have no connection with their military service. The implication is, in other words, that existing VA hospital capacity far exceeds what is required to provide for the medical needs of those veterans with legitimate service-connected disabilities. Secondly, far from providing a homogeneous, military type of environment which returning Vietnam War wounded might be expected to find congenial and familiar, these hospitals are filled with civilians typically twenty years older than the Vietnam veterans.

Inequities in Non-Service-Connected Care

Let us consider then the merits of the emergent role of VA hospitals in providing hospital care for veterans with disabilities which are not service-connected. It seems reasonable to assume that the government might wish to provide care to all veterans out of gratitude and respect for the military services they rendered to the nation. Continuing benefits of this kind are the more justified because many of these veterans were conscripted into military service and thus were underpaid while actually serving on duty. Others volunteered at very low wages largely out of a sense of patriotic duty. The government may in this sense be thought to be repaying a debt owed to these survivors of past wars. If indeed it is objectives such as these which activate the wish to provide medical care to veterans, we may raise two questions in this connection. First, are medical benefits distributed fairly among veterans? Second, is the present method of providing medical care the best way of repaying veterans?

Concerning equity, there seem to be three possible norms that might be applied to a determination of fairness: (1) distribution of benefits weighted by the size of the debt owed to each veteran,[3] (2) distribution of benefits weighted individually according to need,[4] or (3) equal distribution to all. Clearly, each of these norms is relevant to some extent. Antibiotics are not administered in equal dosages to all veterans treated by the Veterans Administration— only to those who need them. The service-connection priority associated with an injury or illness may be thought of as a reflection of the deservingness of a veteran. Surely, however, the Veterans Administration must strive to give equal attention to all patients who are similarly circumstanced.

The very nature of the system implies, however, that one of the most important factors relevant to the distribution of these benefits is almost completely beyond the control of the Veterans Administration and results in distributions which are inconsistent with all of these norms. This factor is geographical location. The Veterans Administration has a total of only 167 hospitals. The number of general medical hospitals in the VA system in the United States is only 139. That means that there is one VA general hospital for every 22,000 square miles in the continental United States. There are none in Alaska or Hawaii. Of the 80,903 patients in VA hospitals reported for October 1971, 13,865 (17.0 percent) were residents of states other than the one in which they were hospitalized.[5]

Regardless of a patient's need or merit, one of the chief factors influencing his ability to take advantage of medical benefits offered by the Veterans Administration is his proximity to a VA medical facility. Although the Veterans Administration since the end of World War II has made a concerted effort to locate its new hospitals in areas accessible to as many veterans as possible, convenience and location must continue to pose an obstacle to equitable distribution of benefits. Only 14.6 percent of all veteran hospitalizations take place in VA facilities.[6] Doubtless one of the chief reasons for this low rate of utilization is the distance a veteran typically would have

59

to place between himself and his home, family, friends, and place of employment if he were to enter a VA hospital.

In addition to the arbitrary geographic distribution of benefits, there is a further inequity associated with the varying availability of space among VA hospitals. Because care is provided at a price far below that necessary to clear the market, admission must be rationed on the basis of non-price criteria. Physicians are charged to admit patients on the basis of medical need.[7] Because of differences in the affluence of facilities compared across regions, however, patients with acute needs are turned away in some locations while other veterans with less severe problems are admitted in other locations. This inequity also operates with respect to time. Some patients are retained in VA hospitals with chronic but medically stable conditions while others with more serious hospital needs are turned away for "lack of space." For veterans with extremely severe conditions who cannot be placed locally, space is usually sought in another VA hospital outside the veteran's immediate region. This, of course, exacerbates the problems of communication and separation from family referred to above. Nor can such extra-regional placement be practiced on a scale that will equalize the temporal and geographic accessibility of hospital care for all veterans. A large random element affects the delivery of VA hospitalization benefits as long as availability depends on where a veteran is located and when his need for care occurs. Variance in health care delivery based on these characteristics cannot be considered a desirable aspect of this program.

Inequities of distribution are unavoidable as long as the Veterans Administration continues to attempt to provide hospital care directly to veterans. Also unavoidable under the existing system are the inefficiencies resulting from information biases discussed in Chapter III. It is, therefore, appropriate at this point to explore alternative means of achieving the broader objectives toward which the VA medical system is directed. In other words, we must address the second question posed above—have we chosen the best way of repaying the debt owed to veterans?

Alternatives to Direct Provision

First let us consider the issue of timing. It was asserted above that the operative want activating the government's provision of medical care to veterans is a desire to repay a debt owed to these men in return for their contribution to national defense. One implication of repaying this debt with hospital care is that such repayment is unnecessarily delayed. The debt cannot be repaid until a need for hospitalization arises. This may in many cases be a very long time. Furthermore, some might argue that an equal or greater debt is owed to the families of those who served but failed to survive to become veterans. If, indeed, it is felt that a debt is created when soldiers take up arms for defense, it may be argued that the best way to discharge that debt is to pay them more *while they are serving*. Such a practice would extend such benefits to all who serve rather than to survivors alone. It appears completely illogical to delay repayment unnecessarily for several decades simply to effect discharge of the debt through in-kind service rather than through pecuniary payment.

The second issue to be raised is the reasoning behind selection of medical and hospital services as the medium of repayment of the debt. If the intention is to make available something which veterans need and can be expected to value, this is indeed an unusual practice. For most veterans, provision of hospital services is redundant and therefore of little value. Increasingly, young veterans are being enrolled automatically in union or employer-financed medical and hospital care insurance plans. Those sixty-five and older are eligible for medical and hospital benefits at nominal cost through Medicare. Higher pay, perhaps in the form of a lump sum *veterans' benefit* payment upon discharge, would enable those needing medical care (that is, care not supplied through some other channel) to purchase it directly or through insurance. Those for whom hospital benefits are redundant and those who simply choose to devote their veterans' benefit grants to other things would be free to do so. It is an economic truism that veterans would universally prefer money grants to the equivalent dollar value in less liquid goods and services. In view of the inefficiencies associated with government provision of hospital services, we should expect such preferences to be even more pronounced. If veterans prefer to be reimbursed with money, why should they be given hospital services instead?

Government Hospital Insurance. Finally, we must raise the question of government operation of hospitals. Even if valid reasons exist which justify provision of benefits to veterans in the form of hospital services, these arguments do not extend to justifying government operation of these hospitals. Perhaps in the interwar period when the VA hospital system was introduced, there were no attractive alternatives. Hospitalization insurance was at this time a rare novelty viewed with disfavor by organized medicine and extremely localized in coverage.

In the years since World War II, however, private hospital insurance coverage has been extended from approximately 25 percent of the population of the United States in 1946 to more than 80 percent in 1970.[8] The federal government itself operates a health insurance system for the aged which is national in scope and has nearly 20 million subscribers.[9] If the federal government were to initiate a program to provide medical care to veterans today, there can be no doubt that it would offer hospitalization insurance rather than attempt to provide hospital care itself. This is how it chose to provide for the hospital needs of the aged in 1965.

A medical insurance program for veterans would eliminate the problems of geographical inconvenience and distributional inequity. Veterans provided with paid-up insurance would be free to use a hospital in their community rather than travel to the nearest VA facility as they must do now. Those with demonstrable medical needs could obtain care without uncertainty regarding the availability of space. An appropriately designed insurance system might offer some efficiency gains as well.

Insurance Programs and Quality Inflation. In setting up any veterans medical insurance program, however, certain pitfalls encountered in recent experience with government-provided insurance should be avoided. The Medicare-Medicaid programs, as well as many private insurance schemes, are offered currently on a reimbursable basis. That is, average costs, as long as they are "reasonable," are reimbursed by the insuring agency. This practice has an effect on hospital care which is the direct opposite of the effect of government organization as it was described in the previous chapter. Instead of being influenced to depreciate the quality of care supplied, hospitals which are reimbursed in this way will typically offer care of a higher quality than an individual would purchase for himself.

As noted in Chapter II, Newhouse and others [10] have suggested that "quality" of medical care enters positively into the utility function of voluntary hospital administrators. They thus infer that excess resources are devoted to production of quality. One need not tamper with the utility function of administrators to generate a theory that suggests this empirically appealing result. Although it is not clear that managers of voluntary hospitals will independently place a positive value on marginal hospital quality, there is no reason to doubt that hospital patients will do so.

Competition among hospitals for patients with reimbursable insurance is almost certain to produce quality inflation. The insurance of hospital charges lowers the price of marginal use in all dimensions. The effect of this lowered price on the quantity of hospital days of care demanded (and thus provided) has been widely discussed and documented under the rubric of *moral hazard*.[11] Just as hospitals provide patients who have insurance with the extra days of care demanded, hospitals competing for these same patients can make their services more attractive by raising their quality—that is, by providing additional services in other dimensions, as well. When the cost of this increased quality is borne by neither the hospital nor the individual subscriber who chooses the hospital, over-investment in quality is predicted. The cost of higher quality is shifted from the individual to the entire population of insured hospital users who bear it as part of the cost of being insured. Under such conditions it is predicted that individual subscribers will demand excessive quality and that hospitals will supply it.

Alternative insurance systems exist which do not produce these undesirable results. One alternative is indemnity insurance policies that pay specific cash indemnities for broadly defined items of medical care such as a hospital day or a doctor's visit. Indemnity insurance, because it does not underwrite unlimited upgrading of the quality of these items consumed, does not influence individual patients to demand such improvements. Individual subscribers must pay all costs above the indemnified amounts, and patients are *not* expected to demand expenditure for higher quality than is worth the cost.

A variant of indemnity insurance is a concept called "variable cost insurance," which has been proposed by Newhouse and Taylor.[12] Its primary innovation is that it allows each subscriber to choose the quality of care which he wishes to insure. With indemnity insurance, one obtains payments of a specific amount for each item of medical care purchased. If one wishes to purchase care of a higher quality than that provided by the indemnity, one must pay the full difference in cost. Such cost differences themselves may be sizeable, and subscribers may wish to insure them as well. Variable cost insurance has an ingenious way of providing coverage for the cost differences.

Each hospital is given an expense rating based on its recent cost experience. This expense rating will be higher for the less efficiently operated hospital than for more efficient ones. It will also be higher when the level of quality offered is higher, however. Each subscriber must select a hospital whose expense rating will form the basis of his yearly premiums. Once enrolled, an individual may utilize any hospital. If a hospital is used which has a higher expense rating than the hospital upon which a subscriber's premium is based, however, he must bear the full difference in cost. In choosing a hospital, therefore, individuals are expected to seek hospitals which operate efficiently for the same reasons of economy that influence buyers of indemnity insurance. Because subscribers must themselves finance the cost of marginal quality in the care they use, they will demand the optimum amount. On the other hand, a subscriber has the option of insuring the cost of very high (or very low) quality medical care by choosing, as a premium base hospital, one with the appropriately high or low expense rating.

Summary of Defects. The existing practice of providing medical care directly to veterans may be questioned on three grounds: (1) It is inequitable in that it is more beneficial to those living near VA hospitals than to those who are less conveniently located. The existence of benefits themselves depends on space being available for veterans when and where the need arises. It also provides these benefits exclusively to survivors of military service. (2) Existing practice is inefficient in that recipients typically would prefer payment in dollars (or insurance) to payment in services that may or may not be used. This is true with respect to time as well as to alternative goods themselves. That is, veterans would prefer an *actuarily fair* money payment during their military service to the medical benefits they currently receive from the Veterans Administration and may use only if and when they qualify for VA medical services. (3) Existing practice is also predicted to be inefficient from the point of view of hospital management. Government-operated enterprises dispensing their products at below market clearing prices will probably combine resources less efficiently and produce output of lower quality than firms whose products must meet a market test. If provision of medical benefits to veterans remains the objective of policy here, then the efficiency of these efforts would be enhanced by providing each veteran with paid-up insurance rather than with hospital facilities. An appropriately designed insurance program would influence veterans to seek out providers of these services who operate most efficiently.

Table 10 presents alternative means of rewarding veterans together with the objections that may be raised against each. The current regime appears to be the least desirable from all five points of view. A switch to insurance would eliminate several objections. The inequities arising from space availability and varying proximity to VA facilities would be eliminated as would the bureaucratic inefficiency resulting from government operation of the hospitals. Adoption of this proposal would retain the inefficiency associated with

Table 10

ALTERNATIVE BENEFIT PROGRAMS AND OBJECTIONS

Type of Benefit Program	Objections				
	Proximity inequity	Space-availability inequity	Survivor inequity	Liquidity inefficiency	Operational inefficiency
Existing system (providing medical care directly)	X	X	X	X	X
Paid-up medical insurance to veterans			X	X	
Cash veterans' benefit grant			X		
Increased salaries for military personnel while on active duty					

making payments in kind rather than in money. It also seems to be inequitable from the point of view of restricting the benefits to survivors of military service, while it might be argued that those who fail to survive are equally deserving of additional compensation. Simply raising the salaries of active military personnel is the least objectionable method.

Treatment for Service-Connected Disabilities

The foregoing discussion has focused on benefits provided to the non-service-connected veterans with disabilities. It has treated the provision of hospital care by the Veterans Administration as a general benefit earned by all veterans with their military service. In view of the preponderance of VA hospital patients treated without service connection, this seems to be the appropriate way to evaluate the program. To argue that the objectives of the Veterans Administration is to provide care to war wounded, and that non-service-connected patients are treated out of excess capacity generated in fulfillment of this mission, is to argue that an enormous tail is wagging a comparatively diminutive dog.

Patients with service-connected disabilities do exist and their importance must be discussed, however. Ex-servicemen suffering from injuries or disease contracted in the performance of military duty have a claim to medical care that must be honored regardless of the scheme of general compensation chosen. Let us consider the advantages and disadvantages of the existing practice of providing hospital care directly to these men.

One possible advantage of hospitals operated exclusively for veterans is that they may provide a more familiar and congenial environment for returning servicemen than private hospitals can offer. A second and related consideration is that such hospitals, by focusing their attention on the limited number of injuries, wounds, and diseases to which soldiers are particularly subject, might become more expert in the treatment of these conditions. Third, a limited number of veterans are incapable of the market activity necessary for choosing and monitoring a private hospital and have no family to do this for them. Choosing and monitoring are unnecessary if the government assumes the responsibility of directly supplying the medical services needed by this group.

These alleged advantages tend to dissolve upon close examination, however. As reported earlier, the average age of patients in VA hospitals is fifty-one years. Less than 10 percent of these patients are under thirty-five years, less than 10 percent are Vietnam veterans. In exchange for the fellowship of this group, the disabled veterans in question must frequently give up the convenience and good cheer provided by the close proximity of home, family, and friends. It seems plausible to assume that, given a choice, most would choose to be hospitalized closer to home in a community hospital.

The benefits of specialization are equally questionable. The treatment of mental disorders and alcoholism together account for almost half of the patients remaining in VA hospitals.[13] While economies of scale in the treatment of these problems cannot be ruled out, neither disability is one with which community hospitals lack experience. Indeed, for those mental disorders arising directly from military duty the beneficial effects of a prompt return to the patient's hometown afforded by treatment in local community facilities would probably offset any advantages offered by special veterans' facilities in unfamiliar surroundings.

Table 11 lists the diagnostic categories in which the number of patients remaining in VA hospitals in 1971 exceeded 1000. Excluding the various mental disorders and alcoholism, one has difficulty identifying one category on this list of most intensively treated disabilities which is likely to be associated with performance of military duty. Indeed virtually all are chronic conditions generally associated with advanced age. Clearly any expertise developed by VA hospitals in the areas reported on here provides no special qualifications for the treatment of returning wounded servicemen.

Table 11

DIAGNOSTIC CATEGORIES CONTAINING MORE THAN
1000 PATIENTS REMAINING IN VA HOSPITALS,
20 OCTOBER 1971

Category	Number
Pulmonary tuberculosis	1,526
Malignancy of respiratory system	1,117
Diabetes mellitus	1,215
Psychoses not attributed to physical conditions	20,605
Alcoholic psychosis	1,464
Psychoses with organic brain syndrome (except syphilitic)	3,712
Alcoholism	3,722
Non-psychotic mental disorders	4,106
Psychoneurotic, personality, and behavioral disorders (excluding alcoholism)	5,074
Chronic ischemic heart disease	2,064
Emphysema	1,023
Cirrhosis of the liver	1,007
Arthritis and rheumatism	1,152
All diseases and conditions	81,150

Source: U.S. Veterans Administration, *Annual Report 1972, Administrator of Veterans Affairs,* p. 112, table 16.

Finally, regarding the treatment of those patients incapable of selecting a hospital and monitoring or evaluating the care provided, it may be noted that control of quality can be exercised by the Veterans' Administration even when it does not itself provide the care. The arguments presented in Chapter III suggest that quality of treatment may indeed be maintained at a lower cost by charging VA officials with the responsibility of monitoring the quality of care provided by others, rather than by operating medical facilities. Organization of the delivery of health services may result in deterioration of the quality of care because of the differing costs of assessing productivity in various dimensions. Private hospitals competing for patients capable of assessing the quality of what is offered will not be influenced to provide inappropriately low quality care. The monitoring problem of the Veterans Administration then would be the comparatively straightforward task of ensuring that veterans in private hospitals were not discriminated against in terms of the quality of care they received.

CHAPTER V

VA HOSPITALS AND MEDICAL EDUCATION

There remains to be considered the role played by Veterans Administration hospitals in the training of health professionals in this country. About a quarter of all medical residents participating in AMA-approved residency programs and about half of all third- and fourth-year medical students receive training in VA hospitals. More than 80 percent of the nation's medical schools are affiliated with VA hospitals.[1] Recent legislation has formalized an even more active role for the Veterans Administration in the education and training of health manpower. The Veterans Administration Health Manpower Training Act of 1972 stated that a primary function of the VA Department of Medicine and Surgery was to "assist in providing an adequate supply of health manpower to the nation." This act seeks to augment the output of trained medical manpower by establishing new schools for the training of doctors, nurses and allied professionals. No study considering dramatic changes in the VA medical care program can ignore these elaborate linkages between VA hospitals and the medical education establishment.

Two questions suggest themselves in this regard: (1) We must consider whether maintaining a system of veterans' hospitals is essential to a continuing output of newly trained physicians, and (2) we must weigh the specific merits of expanding this flow of medical manpower pursuant to the provisions of the Veterans Administration Health Manpower Training Act of 1972.

Effects of Proposed Reorganization

Numerous alternatives to the current VA hospital system were suggested in the previous chapter. Although each proposal involved government divestiture of VA hospitals, divestiture policy does not necessarily imply that these hospitals would actually cease operations and thus be lost to their respective communities and medical education. On the contrary, to the extent that these facilities represent valuable resources in their communities, we would expect civic or proprietary organizations to take over their operations, presumably making their services available to veterans and nonveterans alike. A change in the ownership and control of hospitals should not dramatically affect the demand for hospitals. Hospitals which are viable community institutions under the Veterans Administration should remain so under different ownership.

Consider the effects of providing veterans with medical insurance rather than government-organized hospital care. This change implies no decrease at all in demand for hospital care. Nor is any change in total supply implicit in such a policy as long as VA hospitals are reorganized under private or community ownership. A change in organization might result in some redistribution of patients among hospitals, but in most cases, a redistribution would be desirable, from the standpoint of both users and educators. Veterans currently being hospitalized at some distance from home might, under the proposed insurance system, choose a closer hospital. Space thus freed by veterans electing other hospitals would be filled by nonveterans for whom care in the erstwhile VA facility was more convenient.

The opening of VA hospitals to nonveterans would ultimately lead to improvements in the medical education practiced within their walls. It is acknowledged that the existing patient population of VA hospitals is ill-suited to clinical training and medical research.[2] The inclusion of more short-term acute patients, women and children would provide a much broader range of clinical experience for residents and interns assigned to these hospitals.

A substitution of insurance for government-organized hospital care does not therefore suggest any attentuation in the present flow of newly trained physicians into medical practice. Indeed, far more important than hospitals to the supply of physicians and ultimately of medical services, is the behavior of medical schools themselves. Medical training, like medical care, is a multifarious product, a vector of many output characteristics. In Chapter III we discussed how government organization of hospital care can result in a distortion of the relative outputs of those characteristics. There it was assumed that government officials passively transmit information on the vector of outputs desired by consumers. However, the differential costs of monitoring the levels of these characteristics influence bureau administrators to choose to produce them in inefficient combinations. This behavior was shown in Chapter III to result frequently in the production of hospital services of a quality inferior to those produced by market-organized hospitals.

Similar results might be predicted in regard to government-organized medical schools, save for the influence of organized medicine on their behavior. Administrators of state-operated medical schools are predicted to be as sensitive as any bureau administrators to government officials' perceptions of their productivity. In the case of medical education, however, government representatives apparently rely on organizations of medical practitioners rather than on medical consumers for primary guidance concerning the desired program of training to be offered. Graduates of medical schools must pass examinations prepared by practicing professionals in order to be licensed. Medical schools must conform to standards imposed by professional bodies in order to receive accreditation. Clearly, key indicators of administrator productivity relied upon by elected officials are the success rate on medical licensing exams and school performance on accreditation audits.

It has been persuasively argued that members of the medical profession are better arbiters of the qualifications of newly licensed physicians than are customers or legislators. Although this debate is beyond the scope of a study of VA hospitals, it may be pointed out that members of the medical profession are not economically disinterested in the level of qualifications thus established. Indeed, the higher this standard (and presumably the more costly its attainment by students), the higher will be the equilibrium rental price of this training (human) capital and thus the equilibrium prices of the services of these new physicians. In effect, the existing professionals are empowered to set the price of all new entrants into their market.[3]

The direction of the effect of such intervention in the medical training market has been unambiguous. During the period 1900 to 1920, in which most states empowered the medical profession to establish standards for medical schools, the number of such schools fell from 160 to 85 and enrollment fell from 25,171 to 13,798 students. Enrollment did not return to its 1900 level until the 1950s.[4] The standard of training imposed by the profession was far higher than that which customers themselves had demanded and were willing to pay for.

Whether, in fact, such upgrading of medical school standards is a manifestation of professional concern for the health of the public or of more selfish motives cannot be resolved here. One undeniable result of this policy has been that the rising prices of physicians' services over this period have resulted in a substitution of self-care for increasingly costly physician care. The question of whether upgrading of physician training requirements has resulted in a net increase in the average quality of care consumed therefore remains unresolved.

A second undeniable effect of this policy has been to discourage a large number of potential physicians from entering the medical field in the United States during the past half-century. Should it be determined that expansion of the supply of medical services is indeed warranted, those concerned with this policy must consider a relaxation of the increasingly rigid standards imposed on medical schools and students by the profession with the willing cooperation of government.

Federal Health Manpower Legislation

It is widely acknowledged that economics has yet to produce convincing arguments for government provision of any form of education or training. Many would argue on various grounds that government financing of medical education is warranted. The Veterans Administration has considerable expertise in the administration of veteran benefit programs and none in the areas of planning, organizing, and operating medical schools. If the federal government wishes to provide additional resources for medical education, it may extend financing to schools or students themselves via a number of existing programs.

The federal government has in the past decade provided generous financial support to both medical schools and medical students.[5] Various legislative acts provide scholarships and loans to medical students, capital for medical school expansion and the construction of new medical schools, and bonus grants for existing medical schools which increase their enrollments. If indeed expansion of medical education is desired beyond the level provided for under these programs, then it would seem advisable to make available additional resources through these and similar programs. To add to the broad responsibilities of the Veterans Administration the task of overseeing a large-scale educational enterprise appears destined to add inefficiency in the educational sphere to inefficiency in the provision of hospital services.

The enactment of the Veterans Administration Health Manpower Training Act of 1972 nevertheless provides financing for the establishment of up to eight new state medical schools (Regional Medical Education Centers) to be operated in conjunction with VA hospitals, in addition to funds for medical school expansion in association with VA hospitals. In fiscal year 1974, $25 million was appropriated for this purpose. This course appears unwise both from the standpoint of operational efficiency and in view of the questionable advisability of expanding facilities for the training of health manpower at this time.

The Veterans Administration Health Manpower Training Act of 1972 in its introduction "finds and declares" the existence in the United States of a "great shortage" of physicians, other health professionals, physicians' and dentists' assistants, allied health personnel and other health manpower. The "shortage" of physicians is estimated to be "at least forty-eight thousand." Other shortages noted were 17,800 dentists, 150,000 nurses, 8,700 optometrists, 12,900 podiatrists, and 263,000 allied health and other health personnel.

It is beyond the scope of this study to consider at length the ambiguities associated with the identification and interpretation of shortages of manpower in particular fields.[6] The most common definition is associated with the profitability of investment in medical training. It is enough to say here that these shortages have not been demonstrated empirically.[7] A satisfactory method for gauging the more interesting "social efficiency" of additional investment in medical training has not yet been, and realistically probably never will be, developed. In view of the already enormous financial commitment to medical training currently being made by agencies and individuals other than those trained,[8] however, it is difficult to credit the view that there exists a severe *economic* shortage of physicians.

Another definition of shortages uses noneconomic criteria. A series of projections of "needs" for medical manpower has been produced by the Public Health Service and other federal agencies over the past two decades. Typically these "needs" are alleged to be reflected in existing or desired ratios of physicians to the population. Whatever the worth of such projections as indicators of need, taken together they offer a curious tableau. In 1953 a presidential commission reported a projection of health needs and of the number of physicians required to meet those needs for the year 1960. Shortages of health manpower were predicted unless specific programs were undertaken to expand supply. Although none of the recommendations of the commission were carried out, and the ratio of physicians in private practice to population decreased by 10 percent from 1950 to 1960, no identifiable shortages were noted in 1960. On the contrary, the ratio existing in 1959 was chosen as the standard of need upon which the Surgeon General's Committee on Medical Education based its projections for the year 1975, the well-known

Bane Report.[9] This report projected a need for 330,000 physicians by 1975 to maintain the existing ratio based on a projected population in 1975 of 235 million. The number of physicians projected for 1975 was only 313,000, leaving an anticipated shortage of 17,000 for that year.

Actually the number of physicians who are currently practicing in 1975 is roughly 370,000 or well over the need projected for a population of 235 million in the Bane Report. Population on the other hand will reach less than 220 million. On the basis of the standard of "need" used in the Bane Report, a *surplus* of more than 60,000 physicians exists in 1975. Undaunted by such failures and the fact that the physician to population ratio is higher today than it has been in a century (15 percent higher than in 1960), the Public Health Service produced a new set of estimates in 1971 identifying an existing shortage of from 50,000 to 150,000 physicians.[10]

Stocks and Flows in Medical Education

The identification of a shortage, in terms of whatever criterion, is insufficient grounds for increasing the rate of output of newly trained physicians. Any adjustment in the rate of output of physicians must consider, of course, the existing rate of output as well as differences in the desired and actual stock of physicians. Rapid adjustment to eliminate alleged shortages of personnel is a costly process. Expansion of training capacity can result in waste of costly resources when the rate of training must later be adjusted downward after the desired ratio is achieved. The existing rate of output from medical schools in this country alone would supply a steady-state stock of 293,000 physicians.[11] Stewart and Siddayao projected the effect of 1971 federal legislation on the output of physicians to be an additional 2,000 net entrants per year by 1975,[12] thus adding a total of 70,000 physicians to this steady-state stock. They also report that in the 1966–70 half-decade 3,000 foreign physicians immigrated to this country annually.[13] Assuming a productive life of only twenty years for these physicians, they would represent an addition of roughly 60,000 to the steady-state total. Allowing for no change at all in the rate of entry of physicians into practice in this country, the total number can therefore be expected to increase to 423,000. Stewart and Siddayao predict that this level will be reached by 1980.

New Veterans Administration programs are *not needed* to alleviate an existing shortage. If such a shortage does exist, it will soon be eliminated by the flow of medical graduates from training facilities expanded dramatically during the 1960s. The number of medical

74

schools in the United States increased from 86 in 1960 to 114 in 1975. Five additional schools are in the development stage. Enrollment in medical schools increased from 29,614 to 54,000, an increase of 82 percent, over the same period. Because of the lengthy training period for medical doctors, the impact of this expansion on the supply of physicians is just beginning to be felt. Additional medical school capacity, if completed today, would not begin to affect the numbers of medical practitioners until 1979. By this time Stewart and Siddayao predict that the number of physicians will have grown to 418,000,[14] an increase during the 1970s alone of almost 30 percent. As these writers argue, "The present capacity and output of medical schools will, in time, eliminate shortages by almost any definition. There is no need for further increase in the long-term capacity of medical education and the output of new doctors." [15]

In short, the training of health manpower provides little justification for continuing the system of direct provision of hospital services to veterans. Converting VA hospitals to community hospitals poses no threat to medical education. Should the federal government desire to expand the supply of medical personnel, subsidy programs with government participation limited to the provision of financing are preferable to federal bureaucratic involvement in the actual operation of medical schools. The federal government is and has been for a decade heavily committed to programs of financial support for the training of health manpower. Projections of medical manpower over the period of the 1970s and beyond indicate that the supply of these personnel will be sufficient to satisfy even the rapidly growing appetite of the Public Health Service for increased health manpower. The physician to population ratio, the criterion used by the Public Health Service to estimate our needs, will continue to grow and will surpass the ratio thought desirable by the Public Health Service even without implementation of the VA Health Manpower Training Act of 1972.

CHAPTER VI

SUMMARY AND CONCLUSIONS

In this study I have sought to consider the existing Veterans Administration medical system from the point of view of what I perceive to be its ultimate objectives: (1) improving the welfare of veterans, and (2) insuring an adequate supply of health personnel.

Regarding the first of these objectives, it was argued that the existing system failed in three ways to satisfy this objective. First, it is inequitable in that it provides better benefits to some (survivors, those fortunate enough to find space available, and those conveniently located) than to others. Second, by providing benefits in kind rather than money payments of equivalent value, the system is distributively inefficient. Veterans would probably prefer money payments to the health benefits currently received. Third, the system is considered operationally inefficient as well. Veterans thus receive less value for the resources devoted to providing them with medical care in kind than they might under another system. It was predicted that the system would produce lower quality care and produce it less efficiently than privately organized hospitals would. Evidence supporting these propositions was discussed in Chapter III.

Most veterans in VA hospitals are being treated for disabilities which have no connection with their military service. There is ostensibly no reason for operating special veterans' facilities for this purpose. Nor is it clear that care provided by VA hospitals to veterans being treated for service-connected conditions is superior or likely to be preferred by these patients to care which might be obtained in a community hospital. An examination of the case load in VA hospitals reveals little in the way of case concentration likely to develop special expertise in the treatment of duty-related injury or illness. On the contrary, those cases occupying most of the space in VA hospitals are associated with advancing age.

More Equitable Compensation for Veterans

The most equitable and efficient way to improve the lot of veterans is to pay military personnel more while they are on active duty. There seems to be little justification for delaying part of their compensation until many are dead and others are located where they cannot conveniently use facilities provided. Nor does there seem to be justification for making medical care a part of this delayed compensation. If the Congress is determined to provide benefits in the form of medical care, however, it may do this more equitably and more efficiently by providing each veteran with paid-up hospitalization insurance rather than involving the Veterans Administration in the operation of a separate hospital system.

An appropriately designed hospital-insurance program for veterans need not fall victim to the massive inflationary problems experienced by Medicare and Medicaid. Insurance that covers "all reasonable costs" can be expected to have difficulty preventing "reasonable costs" from soaring completely out of hand. Indemnity insurance avoids this bias towards excessive quality but fails to allow subscribers to choose the quality of hospital care they wish to insure. Under a flat indemnity plan, subscribers opting for higher quality service must pay the full difference between the indemnity paid and the purchase price of the care. The variable cost insurance plan discussed in Chapter IV would permit differing qualities of care to be insured.

Veterans might thus be provided with a basic endowment of paid-up insurance, good for the purchase of the level of care and amenities currently enjoyed in VA hospitals. Should veterans wish to insure against the expense of more costly care (for example, private rooms, special nursing, better meals, and so forth), they could do so by paying into the trust fund a premium representing the difference in the cost of insuring these two levels of care. Such a system would retain the essential quality-control features provided by customers' monitoring in a market framework, while financial responsibility for most of the care would be borne by the Veterans Administration.

Regarding the educational role played by VA hospitals, it has been argued that support for expansion of the supply of medical manpower can and is being provided more effectively by the government through direct financial aid to medical students and medical schools. It was also argued that it is far from clear that additional expansion of training capacity is warranted.

Ending VA operation of hospitals need not imply that VA hospitals will be closed and that VA patients will be cast upon already crowded community hospital facilities. On the contrary, VA hospital facilities may be transferred to community or proprietary control. It was argued in Chapter II that proprietary ownership of hospitals is not necessarily inconsistent with the objectives of providing efficient, high-quality medical care. Indeed, proprietary hospitals have recently attracted some praise from government spokesmen and the hospital establishment.[1] Thought must therefore be given to sale of these resources to private organizations wishing to operate them for profit. Such sales would provide a not insignificant part of the trust fund required to administer a hospital insurance program for veterans.

Many VA hospitals are currently operating below full capacity simply because budgetary limitations prevent them from staffing to handle capacity patient loads. Others could effectively use extensive remodeling and modernization for which funds are also lacking. By permitting these hospitals to handle all patients in their communities on a reimbursable basis, revenues would be generated to finance both needs. Under such an arrangement, inefficient hospitals that could not cover their operating costs should be closed.

It makes little sense today to restrict arbitrarily a potential resource for general use (a hospital) to the use of a narrowly defined group (veterans). The training provided to VA doctors, dentists, nurses and other health personnel is valuable alike to nonveteran men, women and children. VA hospital facilities can also be valuable to the public at large. A desire to provide for certain needs of veterans should not foreclose the use of such valuable resources by others. The proposals discussed above will provide for those needs while freeing physicians and hospitals to serve where they can do so most effectively.

The VA hospital system has elsewhere been compared favorably with hospitals in the private sector on the basis of its existence as a "system" rather than being "a random growth of uncoordinated institutions." The fact that some central coordinating authority exists is accepted as sufficient evidence that such authorities are better able to achieve efficient production than private hospitals operating independently. This acceptance is based, I believe, on the earnest conviction that activities of private hospitals are indeed "uncoordinated."

Economists cannot accept this naive view. They see resources in private hands being coordinated by an admittedly impersonal but nevertheless real institution, the market system. Economists therefore approach the problem from a perspective different from that of the social engineer (planner?). This study has attempted to examine and compare the results of the interplay of individuals under two alternative systems—one in which the coordination is supervised by a central authority, and the other in which activity is coordinated by individual reaction to market signals. The results of this examination suggest that in many respects greater reliance on the market-based coordination might be preferred.

Indeed, in Chapter II it was argued that many of the anomalies noted in connection with private-sector hospitals are the result of nonproprietary organization of these facilities. Studies reviewed there support the hypothesis that proprietary hospitals operate more efficiently than either government or private nonproprietary hospitals. To a large extent federal government policy (for example, the Hill-Burton hospital construction program) is responsible for the dominance of nonproprietary organization in the private hospital sector. It must therefore share responsibility for inefficiencies observed there. This is indeed paradoxical, for, as noted earlier, the Hill-Burton program was originally advanced as a method of achieving coordination of hospital investment through regional planning.

The Veterans Administration's View

Discussions of the conclusions and proposals of this report with VA officials yielded two substantive differences of opinion. These gentlemen argued that the model of government enterprise behavior contained in Chapter III was inaccurate, that managers of VA hospitals were not responsive to the economic incentives which they confront, and thus the differences in the operations of VA and proprietary hospitals implied by the model were invalid. They also argued that a free market for the provision of hospital services will not work; the standard paradigm of uncoordinated competitive supply responding to price signals and yielding efficient levels of care was held to be unrealistic for hospitals. They pointed out that the profit motive governs a relatively small number of these institutions, that private hospitals currently refuse to admit many veterans and may be expected to continue to refuse in the future, and that physicians and not patients typically make the choice of hospital. In essence it was argued that the principal hypotheses suggested in this study remained unproven and that proposals as sweeping as those advanced here should be buttressed by proven fact–not by conjecture.

One can respond to these arguments by noting that the current policy which these officials implicitly defend is also based on conjecture. Admittedly none of the hypotheses suggested in the fore-going analysis has been proven, but none has been disproven either. As seems perversely always to be the case in economic analysis, the facts which would prove most conclusive in resolving these dis-agreements over policy were too costly to obtain. In the absence of such facts, the analyst must fill the gaps with his own intuition, and the policy maker must make do with the best informed intuition he can find.

The opinion of this writer, admittedly colored by the economist's prejudice for market organization of economic activity, is that the picture presented here is essentially accurate. First, as pointed out in Chapter III, the results of the model do not depend on greed and lack of compassion in VA hospital administrators. It suggests simply that those administrators who through error, public-spiritedness, con-scientious analysis, devious design or for whatever reason choose to allocate resources under their control in the manner described will survive in their positions, obtain official recognition and advance-ment, and ultimately serve as models for other administrators. All the evidence uncovered in this study which would illuminate the behavior of hospital administrators has been presented. No evidence was found to be inconsistent with the implications of this model. The reader himself must decide how much confidence he is willing to place in the evidence presented and the countervailing intuition of VA officialdom.

Admittedly, the hospital sector is not very competitive in many parts of the country. Where government policy is responsible for this, such policy should be reversed. The vitality of such proprietary organizations as Hospital Corporation of America and Kaiser Perma-nente nevertheless reaffirms my belief that, not only is private organization of hospitals for veterans a feasible option, but that greater innovation and technical progress can be expected as the proportion of the industry in proprietary hands increases.

Concerning the second objection noted above, that the free market will not work, let me acknowledge that providing hospital care for veterans is costly, and that proprietary hospitals may not be expected to undertake its provision unless these costs are covered. We can be sure that those veterans currently being turned away from voluntary and proprietary hospitals are not those covered by gen-erous cost-plus reimbursement insurance. On the contrary, they frequently have no hospital insurance at all or have exhausted the coverage of the insurance they once had. It has not been argued here that the costs of hospitalizing veterans will simply evaporate as a result of the institutional changes proposed in this study. I have tried to argue simply that any program of treatment being offered currently to veterans in VA hospitals can be provided *at lower cost and with greater convenience* to the patients by proprietary hospitals. Unless such hospitals are fairly reimbursed for providing this service, however, they will certainly *not* provide it.

Finally, in connection with the last objection cited above, I can only note that the market for hospital services is not a fantasy. It exists. It is true that we often rely on our physicians to choose a hospital for us, just as we rely on our favorite restaurants to choose the cuts of meat which they prepare for us. It is nevertheless my belief (another theoretical conjecture) that we all eat better under this arrangement than we would if some government official made this choice for us. In any event, Congress has already indicated its confidence in the hospital market by relying on it for the provision of hospital services to the aged and the poor via the Medicare and Medicaid programs. It was not deemed necessary for the government to provide special hospitals for these groups.

NOTES

NOTES TO CHAPTER I

[1] This figure rose to $2.6 billion for the 1973 fiscal year.

[2] U.S. Veterans Administration, *Annual Report 1972, Administrator of Veterans Affairs* (Washington, D.C.: U.S. Government Printing Office, 1973), p. 13.

[3] There are, of course, statistical indicators such as mortality rates and malpractice suits that measure some dimensions of quality.

[4] Martin S. Feldstein, "The Welfare Loss of Excess Health Insurance," *Journal of Political Economy*, vol. 81 (March-April 1973), p. 269, estimates that overspending of this type on quality amounted to between $2.4 billion and $3.7 billion out of total nongovernmental expenditures on hospital care (approximately $11 billion) in 1969.

[5] U.S. Congress, House of Representatives, Committee on Veterans' Affairs, *Veterans Administration Summary of Medical Programs: Preliminary, June 1972*, Washington, D.C.

[6] American Hospital Association, *Hospitals: Guide Issue*, vol. 47 (August 1973), p. 416.

[7] U.S. Congress, House of Representatives, Subcommittee on Hospitals of the Committee on Veterans' Affairs, *Veterans Administration Hospital Funding and Personnel Needs*, 91st Congress, 2d session, 1970, p. 3347.

[8] U.S. Congress, Senate, Subcommittee on Health and Hospitals of the Committee on Veterans' Affairs, *Oversight of VA Hospital Crisis*, 92d Congress, 1st session, 1971, p. 126.

[9] Ibid., p. 97.

[10] U.S. Congress, House of Representatives, *Operations of Veterans Administration Hospital and Medical Program*, House Committee Print No. 1, 92d Congress, 1st session, 17 February 1971, pp. 244-303.

[11] U.S. Congress, House of Representatives, Subcommittee of the Committee on Appropriations, *HUD-Space-Science Appropriations for 1972*, 92d Congress, 1st session, 1971, p. 67.

[12] Computed from data in U.S. House of Representatives, *Operations of VA Hospital Program*, p. 87.

[13] *Hospitals: Guide Issue*, vol. 45 (August 1971), p. 412. Those ratios are not perfectly comparable, because more administrative personnel are included in voluntary hospital statistics.

[14] U.S. Congress, House of Representatives, *Operations of VA Hospital Program*, p. 87.

[15] U.S. Congress, Senate, Subcommittee on Veterans' Affairs, *Oversight of Medical Care of Veterans Wounded in Vietnam*, 91st Congress, 2d session, Part 2, 1970, p. 603.

[16] Ibid., pp. 707, 708, 740.

[17] Ibid., pp. 707, 709, 710, 727.

[18] Ibid., p. 710.

[19] U.S. Congress, Senate, Subcommittee on Health and Hospitals of the Committee on Veterans' Affairs, *Oversight of VA Hospital Crisis*, pp. 171-74.

[20] Ibid., pp. 236 and 174.

[21] U.S. Congress, Senate, *Oversight of Medical Care*, p. 905. Unfortunately, the written reports of the task-force findings were not prepared until after Senator Cranston had relayed to the Appropriations Committee on 27 May 1970 the unsubstantiated charges made to his subcommittee.

[22] U.S. Congress, Senate, *Oversight of VA Hospital Crisis*, p. 249.
[23] U.S. Congress, Senate, *Oversight of Medical Care*, pp. 856-61.
[24] Ibid., p. 869.

NOTES TO CHAPTER II

[1] Kenneth Arrow, "Uncertainty and the Welfare Economics of Medical Care," *American Economic Review*, vol. 53 (December 1963), p. 950.

[2] Herbert E. Klarman, *The Economics of Health* (New York: Columbia University Press, 1965), p. 114.

[3] See, for example, the broadside delivered at such "skimming" by proprietaries in Roger Rapoport, "A Candle for St. Greed's," *Harper's*, December 1972, pp. 70-75. See also Richard L. Johnson, "How to Make Competition Fair: Have the Same Rules for All Hospitals," *Modern Hospital*, December 1969, p. 104ff.

[4] Joseph P. Newhouse and Jan P. Acton, "Compulsory Health Planning Laws and National Health Insurance," in Clark C. Havighurst, ed., *Regulating Health Facilities Construction* (Washington, D.C.: American Enterprise Institute for Public Policy Research, 1974), pp. 217-32.

[5] Ibid., p. 230.

[6] Arrow, "Uncertainty and the Welfare Economics of Medical Care," p. 953.

[7] This informational role of advertising is developed by Phil Nelson, "Information and Consumer Behavior," *Journal of Political Economy*, vol. 78 (March-April 1970), pp. 257-67.

[8] See, for example, Herman M. Somers and Anne R. Somers, *Medicare and the Hospitals* (Washington, D. C.: Brookings Institution, 1967), chapter 9. Also see *Building a National Health-Care System* (New York: Committee for Economic Development, 1973), pp. 28-44.

[9] Somers and Somers, *Medicare and the Hospitals*, pp. 220-25; P. L. 93-641.

[10] Joseph P. Newhouse, "Toward a Theory of Nonprofit Institutions: An Economic Model of a Hospital," *American Economic Review*, vol. 60 (March 1970), pp. 69-73.

[11] Ibid., p. 66.

[12] Cotton M. Lindsay, "Supply Response to Public Financing of Medical Care in the United States" (Ph.D. diss., Department of Economics, University of Virginia, 1968).

[13] The argument here is that the medical profession uses training costs as a rationing mechanism to limit entry. As all share in the rewards of increasing standards for entry into the profession, there is reason to expect that the level of these standards is "too high." See *ibid.*, chapter 7 and also C. M. Lindsay, "Real Returns to Medical Education," *The Journal of Human Resources*, vol. 8 (Summer 1973), pp. 331-48.

[14] Irwin Workstein reports that in 1963 the proportion of capital spending by nonfederal short-term hospitals in the United States from philanthropic sources was 38 percent. For obvious reasons, this proportion was probably considerably larger for voluntaries alone. Cited in Somers and Somers, *Medicare and the Hospitals*, p. 211.

[15] Mark Pauly and Michael Redisch, "The Not-For-Profit Hospital as a Physicians' Cooperative," *American Economic Review*, vol. 63 (March 1973), pp. 87-99.

[16] Benjamin Ward, "The Firm in Illiria: Market Syndicalism," *American Economic Review*, vol. 48 (September 1958), pp. 566-89; Evsey Domar, "The Soviet Collective Farm as a Producer Cooperative," *American Economic Review*, vol. 56 (September 1966), pp. 734-57; and Walter Oi and E. Clayton, "A Peasant's View of a Soviet Collective Farm," *American Economic Review*, vol. 58 (March 1968), pp. 37-59.

[17] Admission to the staff of closed-staff hospitals is governed by existing members of the medical staff of these hospitals.

[18] Imperfect cooperation among the medical partnership is alleged to imply that resources will be overused. It is quite true, as they argue, that, as each doctor bears only a fraction of the cost of hiring an additional unit of a resource, each will *wish* to employ these resources to the point where the marginal product of that resource to him is worth less than its cost to the whole partnership. This does *not* imply that the entire membership in concert will agree to provide this *excess* level of resources for individual partners to use, however. On the contrary it simply implies that excess demand for factors will exist within the hospitals which must be rationalized through adoption of formal operating procedures or something to this effect.

[19] Kenneth W. Clarkson, "Property Rights, Institutional Constraints, and Individual Behavior: An Application to Short Term General Hospitals" (Ph.D. diss., Department of Economics, University of California, Los Angeles, 1971). See also Clarkson's "Some Implications of Property Rights in Hospital Management," *Journal of Law and Economics,* vol. 15 (October 1972), pp. 363-84.

[20] Both of these differences were found to be significant at the 2.5 percent level. Clarkson, *Property Rights and Individual Behavior,* pp. 52-53.

[21] Ibid., appendix C.

[22] This difference was found to be significant at the 1 percent level. Ibid., p. 66.

[23] See, for example, Somers and Somers, *Medicare and the Hospitals,* chapter 9.

[24] Newhouse and Acton, "Compulsory Health Planning Laws," p. 8.

[25] Robert G. Evans, "Efficiency Incentives in Hospital Reimbursement" (Ph.D. diss., Department of Economics, Harvard University, 1970); Gerald Rosenthal, *The Demand for General Hospital Facilities* (Chicago: American Hospital Association, 1964); J. Joel May, *Health Planning: Its Past and Potential* (Chicago: Center for Health Administration Studies, 1967).

[26] May, *Health Planning.* Similar findings are reported in May's "The Impact of Health Planning on the Hospital Industry," a paper presented at the American Economic Association meetings, San Francisco, Calif. (December 1974).

[27] George J. Stigler and Claire Friedland, "What Can Regulators Regulate? The Case of Electricity," *Journal of Law and Economics,* vol. 5 (October 1962), pp. 1-16; George J. Stigler, "The Theory of Economic Regulation," *Bell Journal of Economics and Management Science,* vol. 2 (Spring 1971), pp. 3-21; Paul W. McAvoy, "The Effectiveness of the Federal Power Commission," *Bell Journal of Economics and Management Science,* vol. 1 (Autumn 1970), pp. 271-303; George W. Hilton, "The Basic Behavior of Regulatory Commissions," *American Economic Review Proceedings,* vol. 62 (May 1972), pp. 47-54.

NOTES TO CHAPTER III

[1] See, for example, W. J. Baumol and W. G. Bowen, "On the Performing Arts: The Anatomy of Their Economic Problems," *American Economic Review,* vol. 55 (May 1965), pp. 495-502, and Joseph P. Newhouse, "Toward a Theory of Nonprofit Institutions: An Economic Model of a Hospital," *American Economic Review,* vol. 60 (March 1970), pp. 64-74.

[2] See, for example, the amusing anecdotes concerning the Soviet Union's experience with "plan fulfillment" in Alec Nove's "Some Problems of 'Success Indicators' in Soviet Industry," *Economica,* vol. 25 (January 1958), p. 1ff and chapter 6 of his *The Soviet Economy* (New York: Frederick A. Praeger, 1965).

[3] See, for example, U.S. Congress, Senate, *Oversight of Medical Care of Veterans Wounded in Vietnam,* pp. 603, 617ff.

[4] This ploy, of course, may be countered with the demand for yet another report, this on the average payment to each category of input coupled with minimum levels to be paid for each. This may in fact explain why one observes strict salary schedules for staff of government bureaus more frequently than for employees of firms. Government managers free to hire staff at *any* wage would be expected to substitute low for high quality staff in order to reduce average cost. A wage floor shifts the incentive to finding the highest qualified individual at the specified wage.

[5] Data supplied by Controller's Office, Veterans Administration. A 5 percent increase, effective in October 1975, has increased the maximum salary to $37,800.

[6] U.S. Social Security Administration, Department of Health, Education, and Welfare, *Income of Physicians, Osteopaths, and Dentists from Professional Practice 1965-69,* by Marcus S. Goldstein, Office of Research and Statistics; Staff paper no. 12 (1973), p. 22.

[7] Center for Health Services Research and Development, *The Profile of Medical Practice* (Chicago: American Medical Association, 1972), p. 70.

[8] U.S. Congress, House of Representatives, *HUD-Space-Science Appropriations for 1971,* 92d Congress, 1st session, 1970, p. 440.

[9] U.S. Congress, House of Representatives, *Operations of Veterans Administration Hospital and Medical Program,* House Committee Reprint No. 1, 92d Congress, 1st session, 17 February 1971, p. 283.

[10] U.S. Congress, Senate, Subcommittee on Health and Hospitals of the Committee on Veterans' Affairs, *Oversight of VA Hospital Crisis,* 92d Congress, 1st session, 1971, p. 163.

[11] U.S., General Accounting Office, *Better Use of Outpatient Services and Nursing Care Bed Facilities Could Improve Health Care Delivery to Veterans,* Report to the Congress by the Comptroller General of the United States, 11 April 1973, p. 23.

[12] Ibid., p. 23.

[13] Ibid., p. 15.

[14] Ibid., p. 15.

[15] Ibid., p. 15 supra.

[16] Ibid., p. 21ff.

[17] U.S., Public Health Service, National Center for Health Statistics, Department of Health, Education, and Welfare, *Illness, Disability, and Hospitalization Among Veterans, United States, July 1957-June 1961,* ser. 10, no. 14 (1965), p. 25.

[18] The Joint Commission is an independent body composed of representatives from the American College of Surgeons, the American College of Physicians, the American Medical Association, and the American Hospital Association.

[19] General Accounting Office, *Better Use of Outpatient Services,* p. 19.

[20] Ibid.

[21] Kenneth Clarkson, *Property Rights.*

[22] General Accounting Office, *Better Use of Outpatient Services,* p. 14.

NOTES TO CHAPTER IV

[1] U.S. Veterans Administration, *Annual Report 1972,* p. 120, table 20.

[2] The analogous percentage of *discharges* from VA hospitals is even lower, that is, 13.8 percent. Calculations in terms of patients remaining offer a better cross-section of VA hospital workloads than discharges, however. It reflects the proportion of various categories of patients actually in the hospitals at any one point in time.

[3] Some variables important in such an assessment might be branch and length of service, type of duty, exposure to war zones, valor at arms, rank, and pay.

[4] Need in this case might be said to be demonstrated by wealth, severity of injury or illness, age, family size, and eligibility for similar benefits from other sources.

[5] U.S. Veterans Administration, *Annual Report 1972*, p. 108.

[6] U.S. Department of Health, Education, and Welfare, Public Health Service, National Center for Health Statistics, *Illness, Disability, and Hospitalization Among Veterans, United States, July 1957-1961*, ser. 10, no. 14 (1965), p. 18.

[7] The Veterans Administration reported recently that 38 percent of those veterans applying for admission to VA hospitals are denied admission. See *HUD-Space-Science Appropriations for 1972*, p. 83.

[8] Marjorie Smith Mueller, "Private Health Insurance in 1969: A Review," *Social Security Bulletin*, vol. 34 (February 1971), p. 7.

[9] U.S. Social Security Administration, Office of Research and Statistics, "Health Insurance for the Aged: Number of Persons Insured, July 1, 1969," Health Insurance Statistics HI-24 (19 February 1971).

[10] Joseph P. Newhouse, "Toward a Theory of Nonprofit Institutions: An Economic Model of a Hospital," *American Economic Review*, vol. 60 (March 1970), pp. 64-74. See also Martin S. Feldstein, "Hospital Cost Inflation: A Study of Nonprofit Price Dynamics," *American Economic Review*, vol. 61 (December 1971), pp. 853-72. Feldstein assumes that quality is an arbitrary choice variable of hospital managers.

[11] This term apparently entered the economic literature on insurance via Mark Pauly's "The Economics of Moral Hazard: Comment," *American Economic Review*, June 1968, pp. 531-37.

[12] Joseph P. Newhouse and Vincent Taylor, "The Subsidy Problem in Hospital Insurance," *Journal of Business* (October 1970), pp. 452-56.

[13] U.S. Veterans Administration, *Annual Report 1972*, p. 112, Table 16.

NOTES TO CHAPTER V

[1] Sar A. Levitan and Karen A. Cleary, *Old Wars Remain Unfinished: The Veteran Benefits System* (Baltimore: Johns Hopkins University Press, 1973), p. 81.

[2] See, for example, Levitan and Cleary, *Old Wars Remain Unfinished*, p. 81.

[3] For a somewhat more elaborate discussion of this see Cotton M. Lindsay, "Real Returns to Medical Education," *Journal of Human Resources*, vol. 8 (Summer 1973), pp. 331-48.

[4] U.S. Department of Health, Education, and Welfare, Public Health Service, *Health Manpower Source Book: Section 9, Physicians, Dentists and Professional Nurses* (1959), p. 9.

[5] The Health Profession Education Act of 1963 (P.L. 88-129), the Nurse Training Act of 1964 (P.L. 88-581), Health Professions Educational Assistance Amendments (P.L. 89-290), the Allied Health Professions Personnel Training Act (P.L. 89-751), the Health Manpower Act of 1968 (P.L. 90-490), the Comprehensive Health Manpower Training Act (P.L. 92-157 in 1971) and the Nurse Training Act (P.L. 92-158).

[6] See W. Lee Hansen, " 'Shortage' and Investment in Health Manpower," in *The Economics of Health and Medical Care* (Ann Arbor: University of Michigan Press, 1964), pp. 75-91. See also Cotton M. Lindsay, *Supply Response*, chapters 6 and 7.

[7] See Cotton M. Lindsay, "Real Returns to Medical Education," *Journal of Human Resources*, vol. 8 (Summer 1973), pp. 331-48, for estimates of the profitability of medical training in 1966 and earlier years.

[8] The Carnegie Commission on Higher Education reports that tuition and fees accounted for only 4 percent of medical school operating funds in 1967-68. See Rashi Fein and Gerald I. Weber, *Financing Medical Education* (New York: McGraw-Hill, 1971), p. 58.

[9] U.S. Department of Health, Education, and Welfare, Public Health Service, *Physicians for a Growing America,* Washington, D. C., 1959.

[10] U.S. Congress, House of Representatives, Subcommittee on Interstate and Foreign Commerce, *Health Professions Education Assistance Amendments of 1971,* 92d Congress, 1st session, 1971, p. 992.

[11] Assuming a working life of thirty-five years for physicians. New graduates of American medical schools totaled 8,367 in 1970.

[12] Charles T. Stewart, Jr. and Corazon M. Siddayao, *Increasing the Supply of Medical Personnel: Needs and Alternatives* (Washington, D. C.: American Enterprise Institute for Public Policy Research, 1973), p. 26.

[13] The annual number of immigrant physicians has since grown to nearly 6,000 in 1971 and to over 7,000 in 1972.

[14] Stewart and Siddayao, *Increasing the Supply of Medical Personnel,* p. 25.

[15] Ibid., p. 36.

NOTES TO CHAPTER VI

[1] Stuart Auerbach, "Hospitals-for-Profit Grow," *Washington Post,* 29 April 1974.